AI Benefits on Your Daily Living

T.C. Catz
AI Benefits on Your Daily Living

Published by Spines
ISBN: 979-8-89569-742-9

AI Benefits on Your Daily Living

T.C. Catz

Contents

Dedication

This book is dedicated to all those who dare to dream of a future where machines and humans work together to create a brighter tomorrow. May this journey into the world of Artificial Intelligence inspire you to explore its possibilities, embrace its challenges, and shape its path for the betterment of all.

PREFACE

In a world brimming with technological marvels, Artificial Intelligence (AI) stands out as a force that's reshaping our lives and redefining our future. From the seemingly mundane (like recommending a movie on streaming services) to the profoundly transformative (like aiding in medical diagnoses or powering self-driving cars), AI is woven into the fabric of our daily experiences.

This book aims to demystify AI, making it accessible to a broad audience. Whether you're a curious individual seeking to understand the buzz surrounding AI, a professional eager to leverage its power in your field, or a student taking your first steps into the world of technology, this book is for you.

Our journey will delve into the heart of AI, exploring its origins, foundational concepts, and diverse applications.

We'll unravel the magic behind machine learning, deep learning, and natural language processing, revealing the intelligence hidden within algorithms and the potential they hold to revolutionize industries and solve complex problems.

Throughout our exploration, we'll prioritize clarity and accessibility. We'll use engaging examples, real-world case studies, and interactive elements to illuminate the path of understanding. We'll also address the ethical and societal implications of AI, encouraging critical thinking and responsible innovation.

This is not just a book about AI – it's an invitation to explore a world of possibilities, to engage with the future, and to become a part of the ongoing conversation about how AI will shape our world. So, let's embark on this adventure together, and discover the boundless potential that lies within the realm of Artificial Intelligence.

INTRODUCTION

Artificial Intelligence (AI) is no longer a futuristic concept confined to science fiction novels. It's here, now, and it's transforming our world in ways both profound and subtle.

From the personalized recommendations we receive on streaming platforms to the intricate algorithms that power self-driving cars, AI is seamlessly woven into the tapestry of our lives.

But what exactly is AI? And how does it work? This book aims to answer these questions and more, providing a clear and accessible introduction to this rapidly evolving field.

Imagine a world where machines can learn, reason, and solve problems like humans – that's the promise of AI. This book will guide you through the key concepts of AI, demystifying terms like machine learning, deep learning, and natural language processing. We'll explore the algorithms that enable machines to learn from data, recognize patterns, and make predictions.

Beyond the technical details, we'll delve into the real-world impact of AI across various fields. We'll see how AI is revolutionizing finance, healthcare, education, and transportation, and we'll explore its potential to address complex challenges like climate change and poverty.

This journey will also address the ethical and social implications of AI, prompting you to think critically about its potential impact on society, employment, and the very definition of humanity. We'll explore the importance of responsible AI development, ensuring that this powerful technology serves humanity and creates a better future for all.

This book is your guide to understanding AI, its applications, and its potential. It's an invitation to join the conversation about this transformative technology and to contribute to its responsible and ethical development. So, let's begin our exploration of the fascinating world of Artificial Intelligence.

Why The N.E.R.D.Y. Way?

The **N.E.R.D.Y.** Way, a potent acronym that stands for k**N**owledge, **E**ducation, **R**esource, **D**iscovery for **Y**ou, embodies the spirit of this book. It's not just a journey through the world of AI; it's an invitation to embark on a lifelong adventure of learning, exploration, and constant evolution. As the field of AI progresses at an astonishing pace, so too must our understanding and engagement with it. The NERDY Way encourages you to embrace this dynamic and ever-changing landscape as a catalyst for personal growth and societal advancement.

Think of it as an ongoing dialogue, a conversation between you and the world of AI, where curiosity is your compass and exploration is your guide. This journey is not about reaching a destination; it's about the continuous process of learning, adapting, and evolving alongside the ever-expanding frontiers of AI. Embrace the challenges and opportunities that come with this journey, for within them lies the potential to unlock your own capabilities and contribute to a future where technology empowers humanity.

The N.E.R.D.Y. Way is a mindset, a philosophy that encourages you to approach AI with a sense of wonder and a spirit of inquiry. It's about recognizing the profound impact AI is having on every aspect of our lives and acknowledging its potential to reshape our world. This mindset fosters a deep appreciation for the transformative power of AI while also recognizing the critical need for responsible development and deployment. It's about understanding the intricate workings of AI systems, their strengths, and limitations, and using this knowledge to make informed decisions about their use.

The N.E.R.D.Y. Way isn't just about acquiring knowledge; it's about applying it to create a better future. This journey is about using your understanding of AI to solve global challenges, foster collaboration between humans and machines, and shape a future where technology serves as a force for good. It's about embracing the responsibility that comes with this knowledge, recognizing that AI's future depends on our collective efforts.

For those who choose to embark on this journey, the rewards are boundless. You will gain a deeper understanding of the world around you, develop valuable skills, and contribute to a future where technology serves as a force for good. It's an invitation to join the conversation, to contribute to the dialogue, and to shape the future of AI for the benefit of all. The N.E.R.D.Y. Way is a testament to the power of learning, collaboration, and continuous exploration, a journey that will enrich your life and help build a better future for everyone.

The N.E.R.D.Y. Way isn't just about understanding AI; it's about becoming a part of its evolution, a contributor to its progress, and a champion for its responsible development and deployment. It's a reminder that the future of AI is not a distant prospect; it's happening now, and it's up to us to shape it. It's a call to action, a reminder that we all have a role to play in this journey, and every step we take, every question we ask, every idea we share, helps us move closer to a brighter future.

Chapter 1

AI the Birth of a New Beginning

The Birth of a Vision

The seeds of artificial intelligence (AI) were sown long before the term itself was coined. In the ancient world, philosophers grappled with the nature of intelligence and the possibility of creating artificial beings. The Greek myth of Hephaestus, the god of fire and metalworking, who built golden robots to serve him, reflects this fascination with artificial intelligence. But it was not until the mid-20th century that the quest for AI took a more concrete form.

The story begins with the rise of the computer, a machine that could perform complex calculations at lightning speed. In the 1950s, a group of visionary scientists and mathematicians gathered at a workshop at Dartmouth College, marking a turning point in AI's history. The Dartmouth Summer Research Project on Artificial Intelligence, as it was called, brought together pioneers like John McCarthy, Marvin Minsky, Claude Shannon, and Nathaniel Rochester. They believed that the time was ripe to build machines capable of exhibiting human-level intelligence, and the Dartmouth workshop became the birthplace of the field of AI as we know it.

The early days of AI research were fueled by optimism and a belief that intelligence could be fully captured by formal rules and logic. This approach, known as "symbolic AI," focused on representing knowledge as symbols and manipulating them through logical operations. Programs like the Logic Theorist, developed by Allen Newell, Herbert Simon, and Cliff Shaw in 1956, could prove mathematical theorems using symbolic reasoning. Another early landmark was the General Problem Solver (GPS), developed by Newell and Simon in the late 1950s, which aimed to solve a wide range of problems by applying general problem-solving principles.

Despite these early successes, the limitations of symbolic AI soon became apparent. The world was far more complex than could be captured by rigid sets of rules. Many problems, such as understanding natural language or recognizing patterns in images, proved to be intractable for symbolic AI systems. These challenges led to a period of disillusionment in the 1970s, known as the "AI winter." Funding for AI research dwindled, and many believed that AI had reached its limits.

But the AI winter did not mark the end of the story. In the 1980s, a new approach emerged, fueled by the rise of personal computers and the availability of vast amounts of data. This approach, called "machine learning," focused on enabling computers to learn from data without explicit programming. Early machine learning algorithms, like decision trees and neural networks, were inspired by biological processes, allowing machines to adapt and improve their performance based on experience.

The rise of machine learning ushered in a new era of AI research. The field began to show remarkable success in areas like pattern recognition, natural language processing, and computer vision. For example, in 1997, IBM's Deep Blue, a chess-playing computer program that incorporated machine learning techniques, defeated chess grandmaster Garry Kasparov in a landmark match. This victory demonstrated the power of machine learning to solve complex problems that had previously been thought to be within the exclusive domain of human intelligence.

The story of AI, however, is not just about technical advancements. It is also about grappling with the profound implications of creating machines that can think and learn like humans. One of the most important questions that emerged in the early days of AI was: what constitutes intelligence? How can we measure intelligence in a machine, and what does it mean for a machine to be truly intelligent?

These questions led to the development of the Turing Test, proposed by Alan Turing in his 1950 paper "Computing Machinery and Intelligence." The Turing Test challenged the notion of intelligence by proposing a test for machine intelligence based on the ability to engage in conversation indistinguishable from a human. If a machine could fool a human into believing it was another human through conversation, it would be considered intelligent.

The Turing Test has been influential in AI research, but it has also been criticized for its limitations. Critics argue that the test is too anthropocentric, focusing solely on human-like intelligence and overlooking other forms of intelligence. Moreover, the test does not address the ethical and societal implications of creating machines that can think like humans.

As AI continues to evolve, the questions surrounding intelligence become even more complex. We are now entering an era of "artificial general intelligence" (AGI), where the goal is to create machines that can perform any intellectual task that a human can. AGI, if realized, would raise profound ethical and philosophical questions, forcing us to re-evaluate our own understanding of intelligence and our place in the world.

The journey of AI has been marked by both breakthroughs and setbacks, fueled by both optimism and skepticism. Yet, one thing is clear: AI has the potential to reshape our world in ways we are only beginning to understand. From transforming industries like healthcare, finance, and transportation to tackling global challenges like climate change and poverty, AI holds the potential to create a better future for all. However, as we harness the power of AI, we must also be mindful of its ethical and social implications, ensuring that it is developed and used responsibly for the betterment of humanity. The story of AI is far from over, and the chapters yet to be written hold immense promise and peril. It is up to us to ensure that the future of AI is one that we can all embrace.

DEFINING INTELLIGENCE

The concept of intelligence has fascinated philosophers and scientists for centuries. What exactly is intelligence? How do we define it? And can machines ever truly possess it? These are fundamental questions that continue to fuel the field of Artificial Intelligence (AI).

Intelligence, in its essence, is the ability to acquire and apply knowledge and skills. It involves a complex interplay of cognitive processes, including:

- **Learning:** The ability to absorb information and adapt to new experiences.
- **Reasoning:** The power to analyze information, draw conclusions, and solve problems.
- **Problem-solving:** The capacity to devise strategies and solutions to overcome obstacles.
- **Creativity:** The potential to generate original ideas and solutions.
- **Language:** The ability to communicate and understand complex ideas through language.

For centuries, human intelligence was considered the pinnacle of cognitive ability. However, the advent of computers and AI has challenged this notion. AI systems are designed to emulate human intelligence, striving to replicate the cognitive processes that make us unique.

But how does AI actually attempt to emulate intelligence? The core of AI lies in machine learning (ML), a paradigm that enables computers to learn from data without explicit programming. Imagine a child learning to recognize a cat. They might see several images of cats and gradually learn to identify the common features: pointy ears, a furry body, and a tail. Similarly, AI algorithms learn by analyzing vast amounts of data, identifying patterns and making predictions.

There are various approaches to machine learning, each tailored to specific tasks. One common approach is supervised learning, where AI models are trained on labeled data. For example, a spam filter can be trained on a dataset of emails labeled as "spam" or "not spam". By analyzing these labeled examples, the AI model learns to identify the characteristics of spam emails and flag them accordingly.

Unsupervised learning takes a different approach. It involves training AI models on unlabeled data, allowing them to discover hidden patterns and structures. Imagine a system tasked with identifying different customer segments based on their purchasing history. Unsupervised learning algorithms could analyze this data to identify distinct groups of customers with similar buying habits, providing valuable insights for marketing and business strategy.

Another fascinating area of AI is reinforcement learning. In this approach, AI agents learn through trial and error, interacting with their environment and receiving rewards or penalties for their actions. A classic example is a game-playing AI, such as a chess engine. By playing millions of games against itself and receiving feedback on its moves, the AI learns to optimize its strategies and ultimately defeat human opponents.

AI's ability to learn, reason, and solve problems is already having a profound impact on our world. From personalized recommendations on streaming services to self-driving cars navigating complex environments, AI systems are demonstrating remarkable capabilities. However, the question of whether AI can truly replicate human intelligence remains a subject of debate.

Some argue that AI is merely a tool that mimics human intelligence, lacking the true essence of consciousness and creativity. Others believe that AI has the potential to surpass human capabilities, unlocking new frontiers of knowledge and innovation.

This debate is likely to continue as AI continues to evolve and redefine our understanding of intelligence itself.

AI's journey towards replicating human intelligence is still ongoing. We are witnessing the dawn of a new era where machines are increasingly capable of learning, reasoning, and problem-solving. As AI continues to develop, it's crucial to consider its ethical implications and ensure its responsible application. By embracing AI's potential while navigating its challenges, we can harness its transformative power to shape a better future for all.

The Turing Test and Its Legacy

The Turing Test, conceived by the brilliant mathematician and codebreaker Alan Turing in his seminal 1950 paper "Computing Machinery and Intelligence," is a pivotal milestone in the history of artificial intelligence (AI). It's a thought experiment that asks a simple, yet profound, question: Can machines think?

Turing envisioned a test where a human judge would engage in text-based conversations with both a human and a machine, without knowing which was which. If the judge couldn't reliably distinguish the machine from the human-based solely on the conversation, then the machine would be deemed to have passed the test.

The Turing Test, far from being a mere parlor trick, has had a profound impact on the field of AI. It served as a rallying point for researchers and developers, pushing them to strive for ever more sophisticated AI systems that could engage in natural language understanding and generation. It has also been a source of much debate, with critics arguing that passing the Turing

Test is not a sufficient or necessary condition for demonstrating true intelligence.

One of the most compelling aspects of the Turing Test is its focus on the ability to hold a conversation. The ability to communicate effectively, to understand and respond to complex questions, and to exhibit a degree of creativity and wit are all essential aspects of human intelligence. By posing the Turing Test, Turing emphasized the importance of natural language processing (NLP) as a key challenge for AI researchers.

In the decades since Turing's paper, significant strides have been made in NLP, fueled by the development of sophisticated language models. These models, trained on massive datasets of text and code, have achieved remarkable capabilities, such as generating realistic text, translating languages with impressive accuracy, and even writing poetry and composing music. However, achieving true natural language understanding remains a formidable challenge.

The Turing Test has also sparked debate about the nature of intelligence itself. Does passing the test truly signify that a machine is thinking, or is it simply mimicking human behavior? Some critics argue that passing the Turing Test would only demonstrate a machine's ability to deceive a human judge, not its ability to think for itself. They contend that true intelligence requires more than just the ability to mimic human language, but also the capacity for creativity, problem-solving, and even self-awareness.

Despite the debate, the Turing Test continues to be a valuable benchmark for AI researchers. It serves as a tangible goal, a measure of progress, and a catalyst for innovation. The pursuit of passing the Turing Test has led to significant advances in areas such as natural language processing, machine learning, and artificial neural networks.

In recent years, the rise of deep learning has ushered in a new era of AI capabilities, with systems now capable of understanding and generating language with unprecedented levels of sophistication. However, passing the Turing Test remains a significant challenge, requiring AI systems to exhibit a deep understanding of human language, culture, and context.

As AI continues to evolve, the Turing Test will undoubtedly continue to be a subject of debate and discussion. It serves as a reminder that the ultimate goal of AI research is not merely to create machines that can mimic human behavior, but to develop systems that possess true intelligence and the ability to understand, learn, and reason. The Turing Test, while not a definitive test of intelligence, continues to inspire and guide the development of AI, pushing us towards a future where machines can interact with humans in meaningful and intelligent ways.

Beyond its role in measuring machine intelligence, the Turing Test has had a significant cultural impact. It has appeared in countless works of fiction, from films like "Ex Machina" and "Blade Runner" to novels like "The Hitchhiker's Guide to the Galaxy" and "The Moon is a Harsh Mistress." These fictional portrayals have often explored the ethical and philosophical implications of creating machines that are capable of passing the Turing Test, raising questions about the nature of consciousness, the potential for AI to surpass human intelligence, and the impact of such advancements on human society.

The Turing Test has also influenced the way we think about human-computer interaction. The idea that a machine could be indistinguishable from a human in a text-based conversation has led to the development of chatbots, virtual assistants, and other AI-powered technologies that are designed to communicate and interact with humans more naturally and intuitively.

However, the Turing Test also has its limitations. Critics argue that it is too focused on human-like behavior and fails to capture the full breadth of intelligence. Some contend that a machine could pass the Turing Test by merely imitating human behavior, without truly understanding the meaning of the words it is using. Others point out that the test is limited to text-based communication, ignoring other important aspects of intelligence such as creativity, problem-solving, and the ability to learn from experience.

Despite its limitations, the Turing Test remains a valuable tool for AI researchers and developers. It serves as a benchmark for measuring progress, a source of inspiration for new ideas, and a catalyst for debate about the nature of intelligence itself. As AI continues to evolve, the Turing Test will undoubtedly continue to be a subject of discussion and debate, pushing us to reconsider what it means to be intelligent and to explore the potential of AI to create a future where machines can interact with humans in meaningful and beneficial ways.

FROM RULE BASED TO MACHINE LEARNING

The early days of AI were marked by a focus on rule-based systems, often referred to as "good old-fashioned AI" (GOFAI). These systems were designed to solve problems by following a set of predefined rules and logic. Imagine a chess-playing program designed to follow specific strategies and tactics based on the position of the pieces on the board. This approach was successful in solving well-defined problems with clear rules, like playing simple games or performing basic calculations. However, it struggled with complex tasks that required adaptability and learning from experience.

The limitations of rule-based systems became apparent as AI researchers grappled with real-world problems. For example, teaching a computer to understand natural language, like English, proved incredibly challenging. The vast complexity of human language, with its nuances, ambiguity, and context-dependent meanings, could not be easily captured by a set of fixed rules.

This realization led to the emergence of a new paradigm in AI: machine learning. Machine learning revolutionized the field by empowering computers to learn from data, rather than relying solely on predefined rules. Instead of being explicitly programmed, machine learning algorithms are trained on vast amounts of data, allowing them to discover patterns, make predictions, and improve their performance over time.

Think of a spam filter. A rule-based system might try to identify spam by looking for specific keywords like "free" or "urgent." But machine learning algorithms go beyond simple keyword analysis. They learn from a massive collection of emails labeled as spam or not spam, identifying intricate patterns and relationships in the language, content, and sender information that distinguish spam from legitimate emails.

Machine learning opened up a wide range of possibilities for AI, enabling computers to tackle tasks that were previously considered too complex for rule-based systems. Applications of machine learning began to appear in diverse fields, including image recognition, natural language processing, medical diagnosis, and financial modeling.

One of the key breakthroughs in machine learning was the development of artificial neural networks. Inspired by the structure and function of the human brain, artificial neural networks consist of interconnected nodes, called neurons, that process information and learn by adjusting the strength of connections between them. These networks are able to learn from vast amounts of data, identifying complex patterns and relationships that are difficult to program explicitly.

Imagine teaching a computer to recognize images of cats. A rule-based system might rely on specific features, like pointed ears or a furry tail. But a neural network can learn from thousands of images of cats, identifying subtle patterns and variations in their appearance, allowing it to recognize cats even in complex and unfamiliar scenarios.

The rise of machine learning, particularly deep learning – a type of machine learning using artificial neural networks with multiple layers – has driven significant advancements in AI, leading to impressive achievements in areas like image recognition, speech recognition, and natural language understanding.

Machine learning, in particular deep learning, has become a driving force behind the recent surge in AI capabilities, enabling computers to perform tasks that were once thought to be uniquely human, like recognizing faces, translating languages, and composing music.

As AI continues to evolve, the line between rule-based systems and machine learning is blurring. Many modern AI systems combine elements of both approaches. For example, a self-driving car might use rule-based systems for basic traffic laws but rely on machine learning to interpret complex driving scenarios, navigate intersections, and avoid obstacles.

This evolution reflects the increasing sophistication of AI, with systems becoming more adaptive, flexible, and capable of learning from experience. The future of AI promises even more exciting developments as researchers continue to explore new techniques and push the boundaries of what's possible.

A Glimpse inot Everyday Applications

Imagine a world where your phone anticipates your needs, suggesting the perfect music playlist for your commute or recommending restaurants based on your past preferences. This isn't science fiction; it's the reality of Artificial Intelligence (AI) weaving its way into our daily lives. From the moment you wake up to the time you drift off to sleep, AI is quietly working behind the scenes, making our experiences smoother and more personalized.

Let's take a closer look at how AI is transforming our world, starting with our morning routine:

The Rise of the Smart Assistants

The morning alarm clock might seem mundane, but behind that familiar chime often lies an intelligent algorithm. AI powers many modern alarm clocks, capable of learning your sleep patterns and gently waking you up at the optimal time.

As you stumble out of bed, your voice assistant—whether it's Alexa, Siri, or Google Assistant—is ready to respond to your every command. These AI-powered assistants are trained on vast amounts of data, allowing them to understand natural language, answer your questions, and perform a multitude of tasks, from setting reminders to controlling your smart home devices.

Personalized Recommendations: A World of Choices

Next, you open your favorite streaming platform. As you scroll through the endless rows of movies and shows, AI-powered recommendations are guiding your choices, suggesting content tailored to your tastes. These algorithms analyze your viewing history, preferences, and even the choices of others with similar interests, creating a personalized watchlist that keeps you entertained and engaged.

The same principle applies to shopping platforms, where AI-driven recommendations nudge you towards products you might find appealing. From clothing to electronics to groceries, AI helps you navigate the vast online marketplace, making it easier to discover new items and find what you're looking for.

The Power of Spam Filters: Keeping Your Inbox Clean

As you check your email, you might not even notice the silent work of AI. Spam filters, powered by sophisticated machine learning algorithms, are diligently sifting through countless messages, identifying and discarding unwanted emails before they reach your inbox. These algorithms are trained on massive datasets of spam emails, learning to recognize patterns and characteristics that distinguish them from legitimate messages.

This seemingly simple task has a profound impact on our online experience, protecting us from phishing scams, malware, and other threats. Without spam filters, our inboxes would be inundated with unsolicited messages, making it difficult to find the important emails we need.

AI in Your Pocket: The Smartphone Revolution

The power of AI is not confined to our homes and workplaces; it's also in the palm of our hands. Our smartphones are packed with AI-powered features that enhance our daily experiences.

From the camera's scene recognition and object detection capabilities to the predictive text suggestions that anticipate our next word, AI is seamlessly integrated into our mobile lives. Even the maps application we use for navigation relies on AI to optimize routes, predict traffic patterns, and provide real-time updates.

Beyond Convenience: AI's Impact on Our Lives

These everyday applications of AI might seem like mere conveniences, but they are just the tip of the iceberg. AI is already making a tangible impact in areas like healthcare, transportation, and education.

In hospitals, AI algorithms are assisting doctors in diagnosing diseases earlier and more accurately. In transportation, self-driving cars are being tested and developed, promising safer and more efficient roads. And in education, AI-powered personalized learning platforms are adapting to individual students' needs, creating more engaging and effective learning experiences.

AI is not just shaping our daily lives; it's revolutionizing entire industries and transforming the way we work, learn, and interact with the world around us. As AI continues to evolve, we can expect even more profound applications and innovations that will change the course of human history.

Looking Ahead: The Future of AI in Our World

As we move forward into a future increasingly shaped by AI, it's crucial to consider the ethical and social implications of this transformative technology. Questions arise about bias in algorithms, data privacy, and the potential impact on employment.

It's essential that we approach AI development and implementation with a sense of responsibility, ensuring that this powerful technology is used to benefit humanity and create a more just and equitable society. This requires ongoing dialogue and collaboration among researchers, developers, policymakers, and the public, to ensure that AI is developed and deployed in a way that aligns with our shared values.

The dawn of artificial intelligence is upon us, and the future is brimming with possibilities. This book will delve into the complexities of AI, exploring its historical roots, technical foundations, and real-world applications. Join us as we embark on this exciting journey of discovery, exploring the transformative power of AI and its potential to shape the world of tomorrow.

CHAPTER 2

THE FUNDAMENTALS FO MACHINE LEARNING

THE CORE OF MACHINE LEARNING

Imagine a world where computers can learn and adapt just like humans. This isn't a futuristic fantasy; it's the reality of machine learning, a transformative field that empowers computers to acquire knowledge from data without explicit instructions. It's like teaching a child by showing them examples instead of writing out a set of rules. This remarkable ability to learn from experience is what makes machine learning so powerful and versatile.

At its core, machine learning is a process of pattern recognition. It involves feeding computers vast amounts of data, allowing them to identify underlying trends, relationships, and insights that humans might miss. These insights can then be used to make predictions, classify information, or even control complex systems.

Think of it like a detective solving a crime. The detective gathers clues, analyzes them, and looks for patterns to identify the culprit. Similarly, machine learning algorithms sift through mountains of data, searching for patterns that reveal hidden connections and relationships.

Consider the example of a spam filter. It learns to distinguish between legitimate emails and spam by analyzing a massive dataset of labeled emails. Each email is tagged as either spam or not spam. The algorithm then identifies patterns in the spam emails, such as specific words, phrases, or sender addresses, that are characteristic of spam. When a new email arrives, the filter uses these learned patterns to decide whether it's spam or not.

Machine learning is not just about analyzing data; it's about using the discovered patterns to make intelligent decisions. These decisions can range from simple tasks, like recommending a song you might enjoy, to complex tasks, like guiding a self-driving car through traffic.

The process of machine learning typically involves the following steps:

1. **Data Collection:** The journey begins with gathering relevant data, the raw material for learning. This data can come from various sources, such as databases, sensor readings, social media posts, or user interactions. The quality and quantity of data play a crucial role in the success of machine learning.
2. **Data Preparation:** Once the data is collected, it needs to be cleaned, organized, and transformed into a format suitable for training the machine learning model. This involves handling missing values, correcting errors, and converting data into a consistent format.

3. **Model Selection:** There are numerous machine learning algorithms, each suited for different types of tasks. Choosing the right algorithm is like selecting the right tool for the job. For example, linear regression is suitable for predicting continuous values, while logistic regression is used for binary classification.
4. **Model Training:** The heart of machine learning lies in the training phase. This involves feeding the prepared data to the chosen algorithm, allowing it to learn from the patterns within the data. The algorithm adjusts its internal parameters during training to improve its performance.
5. **Model Evaluation:** Once the model is trained, it's essential to evaluate its performance on unseen data. This step ensures that the model generalizes well to new situations and doesn't simply memorize the training data.
6. **Model Deployment:** A well-trained and evaluated model is ready for deployment. This involves integrating the model into a system or application where it can perform its intended task.

Machine learning has revolutionized many industries, from healthcare to finance, entertainment, and transportation. It powers recommendation systems, fraud detection systems, personalized learning platforms, and even self-driving cars.

The success of machine learning hinges on its ability to handle massive amounts of data, extract meaningful insights, and adapt to changing circumstances. It's a field that's constantly evolving, driven by the pursuit of more accurate, efficient, and intelligent algorithms.

BEYOND THE BASICS: DIVING DEEPER INTO MACHINE LEARNING

While we've covered the core concepts of machine learning, the field is much broader and deeper than this brief introduction suggests. There are several different types of machine learning, each with its own unique strengths and applications.

Supervised Learning:

Imagine a teacher showing a student pictures of different animals and labeling them as "dog," "cat," or "bird." This is an example of supervised learning, where the machine is trained on labeled data, with each data point associated with a specific outcome.

Supervised learning algorithms are designed to learn from this labeled data and make predictions or classifications on new, unseen data. They can be categorized into two primary types:

- **Regression:** This type of supervised learning is used to predict continuous values, such as predicting the price of a house based on its size and location.
- **Classification:** Classification algorithms are used to categorize data points into distinct classes. For example, a spam filter classifies emails as either spam or not spam.

Unsupervised Learning:

In contrast to supervised learning, where the data is labeled, unsupervised learning deals with unlabeled data. The machine is tasked with discovering hidden patterns and structures within the data, without any prior knowledge of the desired outcomes.

Unsupervised learning algorithms are used for tasks such as:

- **Clustering:** Grouping data points into clusters based on similarities. For example, customer segmentation algorithms cluster customers based on their buying behavior.
- **Dimensionality Reduction:** Simplifying complex data by reducing the number of features (variables) without losing significant information.

Reinforcement Learning:

Imagine teaching a dog to sit by rewarding it with a treat each time it performs the desired action. This is analogous to reinforcement learning, where the machine learns through trial and error, receiving rewards for desired actions and penalties for undesirable actions.

Reinforcement learning is often used to train agents to perform complex tasks, such as playing games, controlling robots, or optimizing resource allocation in complex systems.

The Future of Machine Learning:

Machine learning is an ever-evolving field, driven by the pursuit of more powerful algorithms, larger datasets, and increasingly complex applications. As we move into the future, we can expect to see machine learning play an even greater role in our lives, impacting everything from healthcare and education to transportation and entertainment.

Ethical Considerations in Machine Learning:

As machine learning becomes more pervasive, it's crucial to

address the ethical implications of its use. Some of the key concerns include:

- **Bias:** Machine learning algorithms can inherit biases from the data they are trained on, leading to unfair or discriminatory outcomes.
- **Privacy:** The collection and use of personal data for machine learning raise concerns about privacy and data security.
- **Job Displacement:** The automation of tasks through machine learning can lead to job displacement in certain sectors.

Conclusion:

Machine learning is a powerful tool that enables computers to learn from data, solve complex problems, and make intelligent decisions. It's transforming various industries and aspects of our lives, from healthcare and education to transportation and entertainment. However, it's important to be mindful of the ethical implications of this technology and to ensure that it is used responsibly and for the benefit of all. As we delve deeper into the fascinating world of machine learning, we'll continue to explore its capabilities, limitations, and the challenges it presents.

Teaching Machines with Labeled Data

Imagine you're teaching a dog a new trick. You show it the desired action, reward it when it gets it right, and gently correct it when it gets it wrong. This back-and-forth process of feedback and reinforcement helps the dog learn the new trick. Supervised learning in machine learning operates on a similar principle.

Supervised learning is a type of machine learning where you, the trainer, provide the machine with a set of labeled data. This labeled data includes both the inputs (the information you want the machine to learn from) and the corresponding outputs (the desired answers or predictions). The machine then learns to associate the inputs with their respective outputs, essentially figuring out the underlying pattern or relationship between them.

Think of it like teaching a machine to recognize different types of fruits. You show it pictures of apples, oranges, and bananas, each labeled with the correct fruit name. The machine analyzes these images, looking for patterns and features that differentiate apples from oranges and bananas. After processing enough labeled data, it learns to identify these fruits based on their visual characteristics. When you present a new image of a fruit, the machine can confidently predict what kind of fruit it is, even if it's never seen that particular image before.

Supervised learning involves two main types of problems: regression and classification.

Regression deals with predicting continuous values. Imagine you want to predict the price of a house based on factors like its size, location, and number of bedrooms. Regression models can learn from labeled data of houses with their corresponding prices to develop a model that can estimate the price of a new house given its characteristics.

Classification focuses on assigning data points to distinct categories. Returning to our fruit example, the machine classifies images into categories like "apple," "orange," and "banana." Other common classification tasks include spam detection (classifying emails as spam or not) and medical diagnosis (categorizing patients as having a specific condition or not).

The power of supervised learning lies in its ability to extract complex patterns and relationships from data. By learning from labeled examples, machines can make predictions and classifications that are often more accurate and efficient than human judgment. This opens up a wide range of possibilities across various fields, from finance and healthcare to transportation and entertainment.

Let's delve deeper into the key components of supervised learning:

1. Labeled Data: The Foundation of Learning

Labeled data is the fuel that powers supervised learning algorithms. It consists of a set of examples, each with a clearly defined input and output pair. This data is essential for the machine to learn the underlying relationship between the inputs and outputs.

For instance, in a medical diagnosis task, labeled data could include patient records with information about their symptoms, medical history, and test results, along with a label indicating whether they have a specific disease or not. The machine learns by analyzing this data, identifying patterns that link symptoms and test results to disease diagnoses.

2. Machine Learning Algorithms: The Learning Engine

Machine learning algorithms are the core engines of supervised learning. They take the labeled data as input and learn from it to develop a model that can predict or classify new data points.

These algorithms come in various forms, each suited for different types of problems and data.

- **Linear Regression:** This algorithm finds a linear relationship between the input features and the output variable. It's useful for predicting continuous values like housing prices, stock prices, or temperature.
- **Logistic Regression:** This algorithm is used for classification problems, predicting the probability of an input belonging to a specific category. It's often used for spam detection, sentiment analysis, and customer churn prediction.
- **Decision Trees:** These algorithms construct a tree-like structure to make predictions. They are particularly useful for understanding the decision-making process and identifying important features.
- **Support Vector Machines (SVMs):** SVMs are powerful algorithms for both classification and regression. They find an optimal hyperplane that separates different categories of data, maximizing the margin between them.
- **Neural Networks:** Neural networks are inspired by the structure of the human brain and are particularly adept at learning complex patterns from large datasets. They are widely used for tasks like image recognition, natural language processing, and speech recognition.

3. Training and Evaluation: Fine-Tuning and Testing the Model

Once you have your labeled data and chosen an algorithm, the next step is to train the model. This involves feeding the labeled data to the algorithm and allowing it to adjust its internal parameters to minimize the error between its predictions and the actual outputs.

After training, you need to evaluate the model's performance on a separate set of data that wasn't used for training. This helps to assess how well the model generalizes to new data points and avoids overfitting (where the model becomes too specialized to the training data and performs poorly on new data).

4. Hyperparameter Tuning: Optimizing for Performance

Machine learning algorithms often have several hyperparameters that control their behavior and performance. Hyperparameter tuning is the process of adjusting these parameters to find the best possible settings for your specific problem. This typically involves experimenting with different parameter values and evaluating the model's performance on a validation set.

5. Real-World Applications: Supervised Learning in Action

Supervised learning is used in a wide range of real-world applications, revolutionizing many industries and aspects of our lives. Here are a few examples:

- **Financial Modeling:** Supervised learning algorithms are used to predict stock prices, analyze market trends, and assess investment risks.
- **Medical Diagnosis:** Machine learning models can assist doctors in diagnosing diseases, identifying potential complications, and recommending treatment plans.
- **Spam Detection:** Supervised learning is used to filter spam emails, protecting us from unwanted and

potentially malicious messages.

- **Image Recognition:** Machine learning models are used to recognize objects and scenes in images, powering applications like self-driving cars, facial recognition, and medical imaging analysis.
- **Natural Language Processing:** Supervised learning is used to understand and process human language, enabling applications like machine translation, sentiment analysis, and chatbot development.

The potential of supervised learning is immense. As AI continues to evolve, supervised learning algorithms will play an increasingly important role in solving complex problems and creating new possibilities across various fields.

However, it's crucial to remember that supervised learning is not without its limitations. The quality and diversity of the labeled data directly impact the model's performance. Biases in the training data can lead to biased predictions. Additionally, supervised learning requires a significant amount of labeled data, which can be time-consuming and expensive to collect.

Despite these challenges, supervised learning remains a powerful tool for leveraging the power of data to solve real-world problems and advance our understanding of the world. As we continue to explore new algorithms and techniques, supervised learning will continue to drive innovation and shape the future of AI.

Discovering Patterns in Unlabled Data

Unsupervised learning is a fascinating realm of machine learning where machines are given the freedom to explore data without any explicit guidance or labels. It's like giving a curious child a box of toys and letting them discover the patterns and connections on their own. In essence, unsupervised learning empowers machines to uncover hidden structures and relationships within unlabeled data, leading to insights that might otherwise remain concealed.

Imagine a treasure chest filled with a jumble of precious gems, each unique in its shape, color, and size. A human observer might struggle to classify them, especially if they have no prior knowledge of gemstones. But an unsupervised learning algorithm, like a skilled gemmologist, can analyze the gems, discerning patterns in their characteristics. It might group similar gems together based on their color, size, or even the way light refracts through them. This ability to discern patterns from raw data is a defining characteristic of unsupervised learning.

One of the fundamental techniques in unsupervised learning is clustering, which involves grouping similar data points together. Think of it like sorting a collection of books by their genre. A clustering algorithm would analyze the content of each book, identifying common themes, writing styles, and keywords, and then group books with similar characteristics together. This process not only organizes the books, but it also reveals hidden relationships and connections between them.

A classic example of clustering in action is the recommendation system used by online retailers. When you visit a website like Amazon, you are presented with recommendations for products based on your past purchases and browsing history. Behind the scenes, a clustering algorithm is working its magic, grouping you with other customers who have similar buying patterns. This allows the system to recommend products that are relevant to your interests and preferences, increasing the chances of you making a purchase.

Another key technique in unsupervised learning is dimensionality reduction. In the real world, data often comes in the form of high-dimensional vectors, with many features or attributes. Imagine a data set that includes information about people, such as their age, gender, location, income, and hobbies. This data set might have dozens of dimensions, making it difficult to visualize and analyze. Dimensionality reduction techniques aim to simplify this data by reducing the number of dimensions while preserving the most important information.

One popular dimensionality reduction method is principal component analysis (PCA). PCA works by finding the principal components, which are the directions of greatest variance in the data. By projecting the data onto these principal components, we can reduce the number of dimensions while retaining the most important information. This allows us to visualize complex data sets in lower dimensions, making it easier to understand the underlying patterns and relationships.

Think of it like trying to capture the essence of a complex photograph with a simple sketch. Dimensionality reduction is like finding the key features of the photo, like the outline of a face, the shape of a building, or the color of the sky, and using those to create a simplified representation that still captures the essence of the original image.

Unsupervised learning also encompasses anomaly detection, where the goal is to identify data points that deviate significantly from the norm. This is like finding a needle in a haystack, except the needle might not be obvious at first glance. Anomaly detection algorithms can identify unusual patterns in data that might signal fraud, security breaches, or even the early signs of disease.

Imagine a bank's system for detecting fraudulent credit card transactions. By analyzing thousands of transactions, an anomaly detection algorithm can learn the typical patterns of spending for each cardholder. If a transaction deviates significantly from these patterns, it might be flagged as suspicious, triggering an investigation. This process helps protect customers from financial fraud and keeps the financial system secure.

Unsupervised learning is a powerful tool for extracting knowledge and insights from data without explicit labels. Its applications span various fields, including:

- **Customer segmentation:** Identifying distinct groups of customers based on their purchasing habits and preferences.
- **Image segmentation:** Grouping pixels in an image based on their color, texture, and other features.
- **Network analysis:** Discovering connections and relationships between entities in a network, such as social networks or communication systems.
- **Fraud detection:** Identifying unusual patterns in data that might indicate fraudulent activity.
- **Disease diagnosis:** Detecting anomalies in medical data that could be indicative of specific diseases.

As AI continues to evolve, unsupervised learning is likely to play an increasingly important role in shaping our understanding of the world around us. By empowering machines to discover hidden patterns and structures in data, unsupervised learning opens up new possibilities for exploring the unknown and uncovering the secrets of the universe.

Learning through Trial and Error

Reinforcement learning is a captivating branch of machine learning that draws inspiration from the way humans and animals learn. Imagine a child learning to ride a bicycle. They don't start by knowing how to balance, pedal, and steer simultaneously. Instead, they experiment, stumble, and gradually improve through trial and error. Each successful attempt brings a sense of reward, motivating them to try again and refine their skills. Each fall, a kind of penalty, teaches them to avoid making the same mistake. Reinforcement learning mirrors this process, allowing machines to learn through interactive experiences.

At its core, reinforcement learning involves an agent, an environment, actions, rewards, and a learning algorithm. The agent interacts with the environment, taking actions based on its current state. The environment, in response, provides feedback in the form of rewards or penalties. The learning algorithm then analyzes this feedback, adjusting the agent's behavior to maximize future rewards.

Let's illustrate this with a simple example. Imagine a robot tasked with navigating a maze. The robot's goal is to reach the exit. Its actions include moving forward, backward, left, or right. The environment is the maze itself, with walls acting as obstacles. The robot receives a reward for reaching the exit and penalties for hitting walls.

The learning algorithm, typically a neural network, observes the robot's interactions with the environment. It learns which actions lead to positive outcomes (rewards) and which actions result in negative outcomes (penalties). Over time, the robot refines its strategy, learning to avoid dead ends and navigate the maze more efficiently.

THE KEY COMPONENTS OF REINFORCEMENT LEARNING

Let's delve deeper into the fundamental components of reinforcement learning:

1. The Agent: The agent is the learner in reinforcement learning. It can be a software program, a robot, or any entity capable of interacting with the environment and taking action. The agent's objective is to learn a policy, a set of rules that dictate its actions in different situations.

2. The Environment: The environment is everything outside the agent. It's the context in which the agent operates. The environment can be anything from a simple grid world to a complex real-world scenario. It responds to the agent's actions, providing feedback in the form of rewards or penalties.

3. Actions: Actions are the choices the agent can make within the environment. They are the agent's ways of interacting with the environment. In the maze example, the robot's actions are moving forward, backward, left, or right. Actions have consequences, leading to changes in the environment and generating rewards or penalties.

4. Rewards: Rewards are the feedback signals that the environment provides to the agent. They indicate the desirability of the agent's actions. A positive reward encourages the agent to repeat the action, while a negative reward discourages it. The goal of the agent is to maximize its cumulative reward over time.

5. Learning Algorithm: The learning algorithm is the brain behind the agent. It uses the rewards and penalties received from the environment to update the agent's policy. It learns to associate actions with their outcomes, gradually improving the agent's ability to make decisions that lead to higher rewards.

Types of Reinforcement Learning

Reinforcement learning can be broadly categorized into two main types:

1. **Model-Based Reinforcement Learning:** Model-based reinforcement learning involves building a model of the environment. This model predicts how the environment will respond to the agent's actions. With this model, the agent can simulate different scenarios and plan its actions strategically. This approach can be effective in environments with predictable dynamics but may struggle in complex or uncertain situations.
2. **Model-Free Reinforcement Learning:** Model-free reinforcement learning focuses on learning directly from experience without explicitly building a model of the environment. The agent relies on trial and error, constantly exploring the environment and updating its policy based on observed rewards and penalties. This approach is particularly useful in complex environments where modeling is challenging or impractical.

EXPLORATION VS. EXPLOITATION

A crucial element in reinforcement learning is the trade-off between exploration and exploitation.

- **Exploration:** Exploration refers to the agent's attempts to discover new actions and their effects on the environment. By trying out different actions, the agent expands its knowledge and learns about the potential rewards associated with each action. However, exploration can lead to suboptimal actions, especially in the early stages of learning.
- **Exploitation:** Exploitation involves the agent's tendency to repeat actions that have led to positive rewards in the past. This focuses on maximizing immediate rewards but can lead to suboptimal long-term performance if the agent gets stuck in a local optima.

TECHNIQUES IN REINFORCEMENT LEARNING

Several techniques are used in reinforcement learning to solve problems and train agents:

1. **Q-Learning:** Q-learning is a popular model-free reinforcement learning algorithm. It aims to learn a Q-function, which estimates the expected cumulative reward for taking a specific action in a particular state. The agent uses the Q-function to choose actions that maximize its expected future reward.
2. **Deep Q-Networks (DQN):** Deep Q-networks combine Q-learning with deep neural networks. They

learn to approximate the Q-function using neural networks, allowing them to handle complex environments and high-dimensional state spaces.

3. **Policy Gradients:** Policy gradient methods learn a policy directly, without relying on a value function. They adjust the policy parameters based on the gradient of the expected reward. These methods are effective in continuous action spaces and environments with complex reward structures.
4. **Actor-Critic Methods:** Actor-critic methods combine elements of both value-based and policy-based approaches. An actor learns the policy, while a critic evaluates its performance. The critic provides feedback to the actor, guiding it towards better actions.

Applications of Reinforcement Learning

Reinforcement learning has emerged as a powerful tool with a wide range of applications across diverse fields:

1. **Robotics:** Reinforcement learning is revolutionizing robotics, enabling robots to learn complex tasks, such as grasping objects, navigating environments, and performing assembly operations. For example, robots can learn to manipulate objects in cluttered environments by interacting with them and receiving rewards for successful grasping actions.
2. **Game Playing:** Reinforcement learning has achieved remarkable success in game playing, particularly in games like chess, Go, and Dota 2. AI agents trained using reinforcement learning have surpassed human champions in these games, demonstrating the power of

learning from experience.

3. **Finance:** Reinforcement learning is being used in finance for tasks such as algorithmic trading, portfolio optimization, and risk management. AI agents can learn to identify profitable trading opportunities, make optimal investment decisions, and minimize financial risk.
4. **Healthcare:** Reinforcement learning is finding its way into healthcare applications, such as personalized treatment planning, drug discovery, and robotic surgery. AI agents can learn to recommend customized treatments based on patient data, identify promising drug candidates, and assist surgeons with complex surgical procedures.
5. **Self-Driving Cars:** Reinforcement learning plays a crucial role in the development of self-driving cars. AI agents learn to navigate roads safely and efficiently, adapt to changing traffic conditions, and make decisions based on real-time sensor data.

Challenges and Considerations

Despite its successes, reinforcement learning faces several challenges and considerations:

1. **Data Requirements:** Reinforcement learning algorithms typically require large amounts of data to learn effectively. This can be a significant limitation in situations where data is scarce or expensive to collect.
2. **Exploration vs. Exploitation Trade-off:** The trade-off between exploration and exploitation is a critical challenge. Too much exploration can lead to

suboptimal performance, while too much exploitation can limit learning and prevent the agent from discovering better solutions.

3. **Reward Design:** Designing appropriate reward functions is crucial for successful reinforcement learning. A poorly designed reward function can lead to unintended consequences and hinder the agent's learning process.
4. **Ethical Considerations:** As reinforcement learning applications become more pervasive, ethical considerations are increasingly important. It is essential to ensure that AI agents trained using reinforcement learning do not exhibit biases or harmful behaviors.

The Future of Reinforcement Learning

Reinforcement learning is a rapidly evolving field with a promising future. Here are some potential areas of future development:

1. **Multi-Agent Reinforcement Learning:** Multi-agent reinforcement learning focuses on training multiple agents that interact with each other and the environment. This area holds significant potential for applications in areas like collaborative robotics, decentralized control systems, and social simulations.
2. **Transfer Learning:** Transfer learning aims to enable agents to transfer knowledge learned in one environment to another, reducing the need for extensive training in new environments. This could accelerate the development of AI agents that can adapt to diverse situations.

3. **Explainable AI (XAI):** Explainable AI aims to develop reinforcement learning algorithms that can provide insights into their decision-making processes. This transparency is crucial for building trust in AI systems and understanding their behavior.
4. **Reinforcement Learning for Continuous Control:** Reinforcement learning is increasingly being applied to continuous control problems, where the agent needs to control a system with continuous state and action spaces. This is opening up new opportunities for applications in areas like robotics, autonomous vehicles, and industrial automation.

In conclusion, reinforcement learning is a powerful and versatile machine learning paradigm. Its ability to learn from interactions with the environment makes it particularly suitable for tasks that involve decision-making, optimization, and control. As reinforcement learning research and applications continue to advance, we can expect to see even more transformative applications in diverse fields, shaping the future of technology and society.

MACHINE LEARNING IN ACTION

Machine learning, at its core, is about enabling computers to learn from data without explicit programming. It's a process of building algorithms that can analyze vast amounts of information, identify patterns, and make predictions or decisions. Think of it as teaching a computer to learn like a human does, through experience and observation. Now, let's dive into the exciting world of machine learning, which is revolutionizing various fields.

Fraud Detection: Guarding Against Financial Crimes

Imagine a world where financial institutions can instantly detect fraudulent transactions before they even happen. That's the power of machine learning in action. By analyzing patterns in historical data, machine learning algorithms can identify anomalies that indicate potential fraud. These anomalies could range from unusual spending patterns to suspicious account activity.

For instance, if you suddenly make a large purchase from a country you've never visited, a machine learning algorithm might flag it as suspicious. This real-time detection helps financial institutions prevent losses and protect their customers from financial crimes.

Medical Diagnosis: Empowering Doctors with AI Insights

The healthcare industry is witnessing a remarkable transformation with the advent of machine learning. Imagine doctors equipped with AI-powered tools that can help them diagnose diseases with greater accuracy and speed. Machine learning algorithms can analyze medical images, such as X-rays and MRIs, to identify abnormalities that the human eye may miss.

Consider a patient presenting with a suspicious chest X-ray. A machine learning algorithm trained on a vast dataset of medical images can analyze the X-ray and identify potential signs of lung cancer or pneumonia. This AI assistance allows doctors to make faster and more accurate diagnoses, ultimately leading to better patient outcomes.

Personalized Marketing: Tailoring Experiences to Individual Preferences

In today's digital age, consumers are bombarded with countless advertisements and marketing messages. But what if those messages were personalized to match our individual interests and preferences? That's where machine learning steps in. By analyzing our browsing history, purchase data, and social media activity, machine learning algorithms can create personalized recommendations and targeted advertising campaigns.

For example, if you frequently browse for outdoor gear, you might start seeing more ads for camping equipment, hiking boots, and other related products. This personalized approach not only enhances the consumer experience but also improves the effectiveness of marketing campaigns.

Beyond These Examples: A Wide Spectrum of Applications

These examples merely scratch the surface of machine learning's vast potential. Here are some more instances where machine learning is transforming industries and shaping our future:

- **Natural Language Processing (NLP):** Machine learning is revolutionizing how machines understand and interact with human language. It powers chatbots, language translation services, and even voice assistants like Siri and Alexa.
- **Image Recognition:** Machine learning is empowering computers to "see" and understand images. This technology is used in self-driving cars to identify objects on the road, in medical imaging to diagnose diseases, and in facial recognition systems for security purposes.

- **Recommender Systems:** Machine learning is the backbone of recommender systems, which are used to suggest products, movies, music, and even friends based on our preferences. These systems power online platforms like Amazon, Netflix, and Facebook.
- **Predictive Maintenance:** Machine learning can analyze data from sensors and predict equipment failures before they occur. This enables industries to schedule maintenance proactively, reduce downtime, and minimize costs.
- **Spam Filtering:** Machine learning algorithms are used to identify and filter spam emails, keeping our inboxes clean and safe from unwanted messages.
- **Financial Forecasting:** Machine learning algorithms can analyze financial data to forecast market trends, predict stock prices, and identify investment opportunities.
- **Cybersecurity:** Machine learning plays a crucial role in cybersecurity by identifying and preventing cyberattacks. It can detect anomalies in network traffic, identify phishing attempts, and even predict potential malware attacks.
- **Environmental Monitoring:** Machine learning is used to analyze data from sensors to monitor environmental conditions, such as air quality, water quality, and deforestation. This information is essential for environmental protection and sustainable development.

The Future of Machine Learning: Unlocking New Possibilities

As machine learning continues to evolve, its impact on our lives will only grow. We can expect to see even more transformative applications in the years to come, driving advancements in areas like:

- **Artificial General Intelligence (AGI):** The quest for AGI, a form of artificial intelligence that can perform any intellectual task that a human can, is a key focus in the field. AGI has the potential to revolutionize countless industries and aspects of our lives.
- **Quantum Machine Learning:** The integration of machine learning with quantum computing could unlock new levels of computational power, leading to breakthroughs in areas like drug discovery, materials science, and artificial intelligence.
- **AI Ethics and Governance:** As AI becomes more pervasive, it's crucial to establish ethical guidelines and regulatory frameworks to ensure its responsible and beneficial use. This will involve addressing issues like bias, privacy, and job displacement.

Machine learning is not just a technology; it's a transformative force shaping our future. From detecting fraud to revolutionizing healthcare and empowering personalized experiences, machine learning is unlocking new possibilities and driving progress across all aspects of our lives.

Chapter 3

Deep Learning

Unlocking the Power of Neural Networks

Inspired by the Human Brain

Imagine a machine that learns and adapts like a human brain. This isn't science fiction; it's the reality of artificial neural networks (ANNs), a fundamental concept in deep learning. These networks are inspired by the intricate workings of our minds, mimicking the way neurons communicate and process information.

Think of a neural network as a vast interconnected web of simple computational units, each acting like a neuron. These units, called "nodes" or "artificial neurons," receive input signals, process them through an activation function, and then transmit the output to other neurons. This process is analogous to how biological neurons fire and transmit electrochemical signals across the brain.

Just as our brain learns through experience, a neural network learns by adjusting the connections between neurons, represented by numerical weights. These weights determine the strength of the connection, and they are adjusted during training to optimize the network's performance on a specific task. For instance, a neural network trained to recognize images of cats might learn to assign higher weights to connections that activate when the network detects features commonly associated with cats, such as pointy ears or whisker-like patterns.

The power of neural networks lies in their ability to learn complex patterns from massive datasets. They can automatically extract features from raw data, such as images, text, or sound, without relying on explicit programming. This capability sets them apart from traditional machine learning algorithms, which often require manual feature engineering.

To illustrate, imagine a machine tasked with identifying handwritten digits. A traditional machine learning approach might require a human to define specific features, such as the number of loops or the angle of lines, for the machine to learn. However, a neural network can learn these features directly from the raw image data. By analyzing countless examples of handwritten digits, the network gradually learns to identify the patterns that distinguish one digit from another. This process, known as "feature learning," is a key advantage of neural networks.

The human brain is remarkably complex, with billions of neurons intricately connected. Similarly, neural networks can be designed with multiple layers, creating "deep" networks capable of learning even more sophisticated patterns. These deep networks have revolutionized fields like image recognition, natural language processing, and speech recognition, achieving groundbreaking results that were previously impossible.

For instance, convolutional neural networks (CNNs), a type of deep network specifically designed for image processing, have enabled machines to achieve superhuman accuracy in tasks like object detection and image classification. CNNs are inspired by the visual cortex in the human brain, and they exploit the spatial relationships between pixels to extract features from images. These networks have found widespread applications in self-driving cars, medical imaging analysis, and facial recognition systems.

Recurrent neural networks (RNNs), another type of deep network, are designed to handle sequential data, such as text or speech. They utilize feedback loops, allowing them to process information from previous steps in the sequence. RNNs are particularly adept at tasks like machine translation, sentiment analysis, and text summarization, enabling machines to understand and generate human language.

The emergence of deep learning, powered by artificial neural networks, has ushered in a new era of AI, characterized by unprecedented capabilities and applications. These networks, inspired by the human brain, are constantly evolving, pushing the boundaries of what machines can learn and do.

As deep learning continues to advance, we can expect to see even more remarkable breakthroughs in various fields. From personalized medicine to autonomous vehicles, the potential of deep learning is vast, promising to transform our lives in profound ways. The future holds exciting possibilities as we explore the full potential of these powerful computational models, unlocking new insights and solutions to some of the world's most challenging problems.

Building Blocks of Neural Networks

Imagine a vast network of interconnected nodes, each playing a vital role in processing information. This intricate web resembles the human brain, with its billions of neurons communicating and collaborating to generate thoughts, emotions, and actions. In the realm of artificial intelligence (AI), we find an analogous structure: the artificial neural network (ANN), a computational model inspired by the biological brain.

At the heart of these networks lies the fundamental building block: the artificial neuron, a simplified representation of its biological counterpart. Just like its biological inspiration, an artificial neuron receives input signals, processes them, and generates an output signal. Let's delve into the anatomy of this essential component, unraveling its internal workings.

3.2 The Anatomy of a Neuron: Building Blocks of Neural Networks

Picture a neuron as a small processing unit, receiving information from other neurons through connections called "synapses." Weighted connections in an ANN represent these synapses, each with a unique weight value that determines the strength of the signal passed between neurons.

Imagine a neuron receiving multiple inputs from different sources, each input carrying a specific piece of information. Think of these inputs as different aspects of a picture: the color, shape, texture, and position of an object.

The neuron then combines these inputs by multiplying them with their corresponding weights. This weighted sum represents the neuron's internal state, reflecting the combined influence of all the inputs it receives.

Now, the neuron's activation function comes into play. This mathematical function acts like a gatekeeper, deciding whether the neuron should "fire" and send its output signal to other neurons downstream.

The activation function is a critical component of the neuron, introducing non-linearity into the network's processing. This non-linearity is essential for enabling ANNs to learn complex relationships and solve complex problems.

There are various activation functions commonly used in ANNs, each with its own characteristics and strengths. Here are a few examples:

- **Sigmoid function:** This function takes any input and outputs a value between 0 and 1, representing the probability of the neuron firing. It is a smooth, S-shaped curve, making it suitable for tasks involving probabilities and continuous values.
- **ReLU (Rectified Linear Unit):** This function outputs the input directly if it's positive and zero if it's negative. ReLU is computationally efficient and has been widely adopted in deep learning, particularly for image recognition tasks.
- **Tanh (Hyperbolic Tangent):** Similar to the sigmoid function, tanh outputs values between -1 and 1. It has a steeper slope than sigmoid, making it more sensitive to changes in input, but it can sometimes suffer from vanishing gradients during training.

The choice of activation function depends on the specific task and the architecture of the neural network. Each activation function brings its own strengths and limitations to the table, influencing the network's overall behavior and performance.

Once the activation function has processed the weighted sum of inputs, the neuron generates an output signal, which is then transmitted to other neurons in the network. This output signal can either activate or inhibit the firing of other neurons, depending on the weights and activation function.

This process of receiving inputs, combining them with weights, applying the activation function, and generating an output signal forms the fundamental operation of a single artificial neuron.

But the true power of ANNs lies in their ability to connect these individual neurons in complex structures, creating intricate networks that can learn and adapt to complex patterns in data.

Connecting the Dots: From Individual Neurons to Complex Networks

Imagine a network of interconnected neurons, each processing information and transmitting signals to its neighbors. These networks can be organized in various architectures, each tailored to specific types of problems.

One common architecture is the feedforward network, where information flows in one direction, from the input layer to the output layer, without any loops or cycles. These networks are well-suited for tasks like image classification, where the input is a set of pixels and the output is a prediction of the object depicted in the image.

In contrast, recurrent neural networks (RNNs) introduce feedback loops, allowing information to flow in both directions. This allows RNNs to process sequential data, such as natural language, where the order of words and phrases is crucial for understanding meaning.

Convolutional neural networks (CNNs) are specifically designed for image processing. They utilize convolutional filters, which slide across the input image, extracting features such as edges, textures, and shapes. These features are then passed to subsequent layers for further processing and classification.

The interconnectedness and complexity of these neural networks allow them to learn from data and adapt their behavior over time. They can identify intricate patterns and relationships within data, making predictions, solving problems, and generating creative outputs.

The Power of Learning: Training Neural Networks

Training a neural network involves adjusting its weights and biases to optimize its performance on a specific task.

This process typically involves feeding the network with a large dataset of labeled examples. The network then attempts to predict the correct output for each example, adjusting its weights and biases to minimize the difference between its predictions and the actual labels.

This process of adjusting weights and biases is called backpropagation. It involves calculating the error between the network's prediction and the true label, and then propagating this error back through the network, updating the weights and biases to reduce the overall error.

The Learning Process

Imagine a child learning to recognize a dog. Initially, they might identify any furry creature as a dog. However, through repeated exposure to different dogs, they gradually refine their understanding, learning to differentiate dogs from other animals.

Similarly, a neural network learns by being exposed to a large dataset of examples. It starts with randomly initialized weights and biases and gradually adjusts them based on the feedback it receives from the training data.

The network's performance improves over time as it learns from the examples, identifying patterns and relationships within the data.

The Importance of Data

The quality and quantity of training data are crucial for the success of a neural network. A network trained on a diverse and representative dataset is more likely to generalize well to new and unseen data.

For example, a network trained on a dataset of images showing only one breed of dog might struggle to recognize other breeds. However, a network trained on a dataset with images of many different dog breeds will be more robust and adaptable.

The Role of Optimization

Training a neural network involves optimizing its parameters (weights and biases) to minimize the error between its predictions and the actual labels.

This optimization process often involves sophisticated algorithms, such as stochastic gradient descent (SGD), which update the parameters iteratively, gradually moving towards a solution that minimizes the error.

The Power of Deep Learning

Deep learning, a subfield of machine learning, focuses on using deep neural networks with multiple layers. These networks are capable of learning complex representations from data and have achieved remarkable success in various fields, such as image recognition, natural language processing, and machine translation.

The depth of these networks allows them to extract hierarchical features from data. Imagine a network learning to recognize a cat in an image. The first layer might detect simple edges and shapes. The second layer might combine these edges to form more complex features, such as eyes, ears, and whiskers. Subsequent layers might then combine these features to form the final representation of a cat.

Applications of Deep Learning

Deep learning has revolutionized various industries, driving progress in areas like:

- **Image Recognition:** Deep learning powers image classification and object detection systems used in self-driving cars, medical diagnosis, and security systems.
- **Natural Language Processing:** Deep learning has enabled significant advancements in machine translation, sentiment analysis, text summarization, and chatbot development.
- **Speech Recognition:** Deep learning powers virtual assistants and speech-to-text systems, enabling

machines to understand and respond to human speech.

- **Drug Discovery:** Deep learning is being used to identify potential drug targets and accelerate the development of new medications.

The Future of Deep Learning

Deep learning continues to evolve, with new architectures, algorithms, and applications emerging constantly.

Researchers are exploring ways to enhance the capabilities of deep learning models, making them more efficient, robust, and adaptable.

The future of deep learning holds immense promise for solving complex problems, driving innovation, and shaping the world around us.

FROM FEEDFORWARD TO CONVOLUATIONAL NETWORKS

Deep learning, a powerful subfield of machine learning, is fueled by artificial neural networks (ANNs). These networks are inspired by the structure and function of the human brain, composed of interconnected nodes called neurons. Each neuron processes information and transmits it to other neurons, enabling the network to learn complex patterns from data.

Feedforward Networks: The Foundation of Deep Learning

Imagine a simple neural network with layers of neurons stacked vertically. Each layer receives input from the previous layer, processes it, and then passes it on to the next. This sequential flow of information, from input to output, characterizes a feedforward network. Think of it like a chain reaction, where each neuron triggers the next one in a specific direction.

Feedforward networks are excellent for classifying data into distinct categories. Consider the task of identifying handwritten digits. A feedforward network can learn to recognize the unique features of each digit by analyzing patterns in the image's pixel data. The network learns by adjusting the strength of connections, or weights, between neurons, ultimately creating a "fingerprint" for each digit.

Convolutional Neural Networks (CNNs): Masterminds of Image Recognition

Convolutional neural networks, or CNNs, are a specialized type of feedforward network designed to excel in image recognition. Instead of processing individual pixels independently, CNNs leverage a technique called convolution, which essentially scans the image with a filter. This filter focuses on specific features like edges, corners, or textures, extracting crucial information for the task at hand.

Imagine you're trying to identify a cat in a photo. A CNN might first detect the edges of its fur, then recognize the shape of its ears, and finally identify its whisker patterns. This layered approach allows CNNs to break down complex images into meaningful components, enabling them to learn and identify objects with remarkable accuracy.

CNNs have revolutionized image recognition, driving advancements in areas such as:

- **Object Detection:** CNNs can accurately identify and locate objects within images, making them crucial for applications like autonomous vehicles and medical diagnosis.
- **Image Classification:** CNNs are highly adept at categorizing images into different classes, enabling tasks like facial recognition, image search, and content moderation.
- **Medical Imaging:** CNNs are increasingly used in medical imaging to detect tumors, analyze X-rays, and assist in disease diagnosis.

Recurrent Neural Networks (RNNs): Masters of Sequence Learning

While feedforward networks and CNNs shine in processing static data like images, recurrent neural networks (RNNs) are adept at handling sequential data, where order matters. Think of sentences in a book, notes in a musical composition, or even the patterns of your heartbeat. RNNs excel at understanding the context and dependencies within such data streams.

A key feature of RNNs is their ability to remember past information. Each neuron in an RNN receives input not only from the previous layer but also from its own past activations. This internal memory mechanism allows the network to retain and leverage previous information, creating a sense of "context" for the current input.

RNNs are particularly effective for tasks involving:

- **Natural Language Processing (NLP):** RNNs are widely used in NLP tasks such as machine translation, text summarization, sentiment analysis, and chatbot development.

- **Speech Recognition:** RNNs can learn to recognize and interpret spoken language, enabling voice assistants and speech-to-text applications.
- **Time Series Analysis:** RNNs can analyze time series data like stock prices, weather patterns, and sensor readings to identify trends, predict future values, and make informed decisions.

Deep Learning: A Journey of Continuous Evolution

The world of deep learning is a dynamic landscape, constantly evolving with new architectures and algorithms. Researchers are continually exploring and pushing the boundaries of what these powerful networks can achieve. From the foundational feedforward networks to the specialized capabilities of CNNs and RNNs, each architecture brings unique strengths to the table.

Deep learning is not just a technology; it's a transformative force reshaping how we interact with the world. It empowers machines to learn from data, solve complex problems, and unlock new possibilities. As we continue to explore the depths of neural networks, we can expect even more remarkable advancements in the years to come.

Driving Advancement in AI

The rise of deep learning is a story of technological convergence, fueled by several key factors:

1. **The Data Explosion:** The digital age has brought an unprecedented surge in data, providing a vast and

fertile ground for deep learning algorithms to feast upon. From social media posts and online shopping records to scientific data and medical images, the sheer volume and variety of available data have created a rich tapestry for deep learning to unravel. This abundance of data allows deep learning models to learn intricate patterns and representations, achieving levels of accuracy previously unattainable.

2. **The Power of Computation:** The simultaneous advancement in computing power, particularly the development of powerful graphics processing units (GPUs), has played a pivotal role in the rise of deep learning. GPUs, initially designed for rendering graphics in video games, proved surprisingly adept at handling the complex matrix operations that underpin deep learning. Their parallel processing capabilities dramatically accelerated the training of deep learning models, making it feasible to process massive datasets within a reasonable timeframe.
3. **The Algorithmic Breakthroughs:** The development of innovative deep learning architectures, such as convolutional neural networks (CNNs) and recurrent neural networks (RNNs), has unlocked new capabilities and pushed the boundaries of what deep learning can achieve. CNNs, with their ability to capture spatial patterns, revolutionized image recognition and computer vision. RNNs, with their capacity to process sequential data, have become indispensable in natural language processing, enabling machines to understand and generate human language.
4. **The Open-Source Revolution:** The rise of open-source software and libraries, such as TensorFlow,

PyTorch, and Keras, has democratized access to deep learning tools. These open-source platforms have empowered developers, researchers, and enthusiasts alike to experiment with and build upon deep learning technology. This open-source ecosystem fosters collaboration, knowledge sharing, and rapid innovation, propelling the field forward at an unprecedented pace.

5. **The Success Stories:** Deep learning has consistently delivered remarkable results in various domains, generating immense interest and investment. From image recognition systems that outperform human accuracy to machine translation systems that bridge language barriers, deep learning has demonstrated its transformative potential across diverse fields. These success stories have solidified deep learning's position as a powerful force driving advancements in artificial intelligence.

Deep Learning's Impact on Image Recognition

Deep learning has revolutionized image recognition, achieving remarkable accuracy in tasks that once proved insurmountable for traditional computer vision methods. Convolutional neural networks (CNNs), specifically, have emerged as the dominant force in this domain. CNNs are designed to process and extract features from images, capturing spatial relationships and patterns.

Imagine a CNN tasked with recognizing a cat in an image. It starts by analyzing the pixels at the lowest level, identifying simple features like edges and lines. As the information flows through the network, these low-level features are combined and abstracted to form higher-level features, such as the shape of a cat's ear or the texture of its fur. Eventually, the network learns to recognize the complex pattern that defines a cat, allowing it to classify images with remarkable accuracy.

The success of deep learning in image recognition has led to groundbreaking applications. Self-driving cars rely on CNNs to interpret real-time images captured by their cameras, navigating roads and avoiding obstacles. Medical imaging analysis, leveraging CNNs to detect tumors in X-rays and identify abnormalities in MRI scans, has become a crucial tool for disease diagnosis and patient care.

Deep Learning in Natural Language Processing

Deep learning has also made significant strides in natural language processing (NLP), the field that focuses on enabling machines to understand and process human language. The advent of recurrent neural networks (RNNs) and their variations, such as long short-term memory (LSTM) networks, has empowered NLP systems to handle the sequential nature of language.

RNNs are designed to process data in a sequential manner, remembering previous inputs and using them to inform the processing of subsequent inputs. This ability to capture the context of words and phrases is essential for tasks like machine translation, sentiment analysis, and text summarization.

Machine translation systems, powered by deep learning, can now translate text between languages with remarkable fluency and accuracy, breaking down communication barriers and enabling seamless global exchange of information. Sentiment analysis, using deep learning to analyze text and extract emotions and opinions, has become an invaluable tool for businesses, allowing them to understand customer sentiment and tailor their products and services accordingly.

Deep Learning in Other Domains

The impact of deep learning extends far beyond image recognition and NLP, transforming a wide range of fields:

- **Drug Discovery:** Deep learning algorithms are being used to accelerate the process of drug discovery, identifying potential drug targets, predicting drug efficacy, and optimizing drug design.
- **Finance:** AI-powered algorithms are revolutionizing financial markets, automating investment decisions, detecting fraud, and personalizing financial services.
- **Healthcare:** Deep learning is used in medical diagnosis, personalized medicine, and medical imaging analysis, enhancing patient care and improving disease outcomes.
- **Education:** Deep learning is being used to personalize learning experiences, provide educational support, and improve student assessment, making education more effective and engaging.

Challenges and Ethical Considerations

Despite its remarkable achievements, deep learning also presents challenges and raises ethical considerations:

- **Bias and Fairness:** Deep learning models, trained on large datasets, can inherit and amplify biases present in the data. This can lead to discriminatory outcomes, particularly in sensitive areas like loan approvals or criminal justice.

- **Privacy and Security:** The vast amount of data used to train deep learning models raises concerns about data privacy and security. It's crucial to implement robust security measures to protect sensitive information and ensure responsible data management.
- **Job Displacement:** The automation capabilities of deep learning raise concerns about job displacement. It's important to develop strategies for reskilling and upskilling the workforce to adapt to the changing job market.

The Future of Deep Learning

Deep learning is an ever-evolving field, with exciting advancements on the horizon:

- **Artificial General Intelligence (AGI):** The ultimate goal of deep learning research is to develop artificial general intelligence (AGI), machines with human-like intelligence that can learn and perform any task that a human can.
- **Quantum Computing:** The potential of quantum computing to accelerate deep learning research and development is immense, opening doors to solving previously intractable problems and achieving breakthroughs in AI.
- **Explainability and Transparency:** As deep learning models become more complex, it's crucial to develop techniques for understanding and interpreting their decisions, ensuring transparency and accountability.

Deep learning has become a cornerstone of modern artificial intelligence, driving advancements across diverse fields and shaping the future of our world. As we continue to explore and refine this powerful technology, it's essential to navigate the ethical and social implications, ensuring that AI serves humanity and creates a better future for all.

Solving Complex Problems

Deep learning, a subfield of machine learning, has emerged as a revolutionary force in artificial intelligence, transforming the way we approach complex problems across various domains. The key to deep learning's remarkable success lies in its ability to learn intricate patterns and representations from massive datasets, mimicking the cognitive processes of the human brain.

One of the most captivating aspects of deep learning is its application in image recognition. Imagine a computer capable of identifying objects, scenes, and faces in images with astonishing accuracy, just like a human eye. This remarkable feat is achieved through convolutional neural networks (CNNs), a specialized type of deep learning architecture designed to process visual information. CNNs have revolutionized fields like medical imaging, where they assist doctors in identifying tumors, detecting abnormalities, and making more accurate diagnoses. They power self-driving cars, enabling them to perceive their surroundings and make safe navigation decisions. In e-commerce, CNNs are used to identify and categorize products, improving search functionality and personalized recommendations.

Deep learning's prowess extends beyond image recognition. It has revolutionized natural language processing (NLP), the field of enabling machines to understand and process human language. By training deep neural networks on massive text corpora, we can now create language models capable of generating coherent text, translating languages with high accuracy, and understanding the nuances of human communication. These models power virtual assistants like Siri and Alexa, enabling them to converse naturally and respond to complex questions. They drive machine translation services like Google Translate, breaking down language barriers and fostering global communication.

Deep learning has also opened up unprecedented possibilities in the realm of drug discovery. By analyzing vast datasets of molecular structures and biological pathways, deep learning algorithms can identify potential drug candidates, predict their efficacy, and optimize their properties. This significantly accelerates the drug development process, reducing costs and bringing life-saving medications to market faster. Deep learning is also being used to personalize medicine, tailoring treatments to individual patients based on their genetic makeup, lifestyle, and medical history.

Let's delve into some real-world examples that showcase the transformative power of deep learning:

- **Image Recognition in Healthcare:** Imagine a radiologist reviewing thousands of chest X-rays each day. This arduous task can be significantly aided by deep learning algorithms that can automatically detect potential abnormalities, highlighting areas of concern for the radiologist. This not only saves time but also improves the accuracy of diagnosis and helps identify early signs of diseases like lung cancer and pneumonia.

- **Natural Language Processing in Customer Service:** Imagine a chatbot that can understand your requests, answer your questions, and resolve issues with the same accuracy and empathy as a human agent. Deep learning-powered chatbots are transforming customer service by providing 24/7 availability, personalized interactions, and quick resolution times. This enhances customer satisfaction, reduces waiting times, and frees up human agents to focus on more complex tasks.
- **Drug Discovery in Pharmaceutical Research:** Imagine scientists searching for new drugs to combat diseases like cancer and Alzheimer's. Deep learning algorithms can analyze millions of molecules, identifying potential drug candidates with specific properties that target disease-causing pathways. This accelerates the drug discovery process, making it more efficient, cost-effective, and ultimately saving lives.

Deep learning is not just a technological advancement; it represents a paradigm shift in how we approach complex problems. By harnessing the power of neural networks and massive datasets, we are empowering machines to learn, adapt, and solve problems that were once deemed intractable. As we delve deeper into the possibilities of deep learning, we are on the verge of unlocking a new era of technological innovation and progress. This progress promises to transform our lives in countless ways, from improving healthcare to revolutionizing transportation, from automating tasks to fostering creativity. As we navigate this exciting new frontier, it is imperative that we develop and implement deep learning technologies responsibly, ensuring that they serve humanity and contribute to a brighter future for all.

Chapter 4

Natural Language Processing

Enabling Machines to Understand Language

Understanding Human Communication

Imagine a world where computers can understand the nuances of human language, where they can converse with us, translate languages effortlessly, and even compose stories. This is the promise of Natural Language Processing (NLP), a field of AI that seeks to bridge the gap between human language and the computational world. However, this journey is fraught with challenges. Human language, with its intricate structure, diverse meanings, and contextual variations, presents a formidable obstacle for machines to grasp.

The Complexities of Language

At its core, natural language is a complex system of symbols and rules that we use to express ourselves. Consider the seemingly simple sentence, "The cat sat on the mat." This sentence encodes information about the action (sitting), the agent (cat), the location (mat), and the relationship between them. To understand this sentence, a machine needs to:

- **Recognize individual words:** It must be able to identify the words "the," "cat," "sat," "on," and "mat" as distinct units of meaning. This process, called tokenization, is often the first step in NLP.
- **Determine word meanings:** The machine needs to understand the meanings of individual words, including their multiple meanings and the context-dependent interpretations. For instance, "cat" can refer to a feline animal or to a tool for lifting objects.
- **Interpret grammatical structure:** It must parse the sentence to understand the grammatical relationships between words. This involves identifying the subject (cat), verb (sat), and object (mat) and understanding how the preposition "on" relates them.
- **Resolve ambiguity:** Human language is rife with ambiguity. Consider the phrase "I saw the man with the telescope." This could mean the man was holding the telescope, or that I used the telescope to see the man. The machine needs to resolve such ambiguities based on context.
- **Comprehend context:** The meaning of a word or phrase is often influenced by the surrounding text and the broader situation. The sentence "The cat sat on the mat" takes on a different meaning if we are talking about a cat show versus a construction site.

These challenges are further compounded by the inherent variability of human language. We use slang, dialects, and colloquialisms, and our communication is often riddled with errors, misspellings, and incomplete sentences. Moreover, language is constantly evolving with new words and phrases emerging, making it an ever-changing target for NLP systems.

The Quest for Machine Comprehension

To overcome these challenges, NLP researchers have developed sophisticated techniques to enable machines to understand and process language.

1. **Statistical Language Models:** Early approaches relied on statistical language models. These models analyze vast amounts of text data to learn the probability of words appearing in specific contexts. For instance, they can predict the likelihood of the word "cat" appearing after the word "the." This approach, while effective in some tasks, struggles with complex language and nuances.
2. **Neural Language Models:** The advent of deep learning has revolutionized NLP. Neural language models, inspired by the human brain, can learn more complex patterns and relationships in language. They are trained on massive datasets and can handle complex sentences, understand context, and even generate human-like text.
3. **Word Embeddings:** To represent words in a way that machines can understand, NLP utilizes techniques called word embeddings. These methods map words to numerical vectors, capturing their semantic relationships. Words with similar meanings will have vectors that are closer to each other, enabling machines to reason about word analogies and relationships.
4. **Natural Language Understanding (NLU):** This subfield of NLP focuses on enabling machines to interpret and understand the meaning of text. NLU techniques involve tasks like:

- **Named Entity Recognition (NER):** Identifying entities like people, places, and organizations in text.
- **Sentiment Analysis:** Determining the emotional tone or sentiment expressed in text, such as positive, negative, or neutral.
- **Text Summarization:** Generating concise summaries of long texts while preserving key information.
- **Question Answering:** Providing answers to questions based on given text.

5. **Natural Language Generation (NLG):** This subfield focuses on enabling machines to generate human-like text. NLG techniques are used in:
   - **Machine Translation:** Converting text from one language to another.
   - **Chatbots:** Creating conversational agents that can interact with humans in natural language.
   - **Content Creation:** Generating text for websites, articles, or social media posts.

The Future of NLP: A More Human-Like Interaction

NLP is constantly evolving, pushing the boundaries of what machines can understand and generate. Future advancements promise even more intuitive and human-like interactions. Imagine:

- **Hyper-personalized experiences:** NLP-powered applications can tailor content, recommendations, and services to individual needs and preferences, understanding your interests and adapting to your communication style.

- **Enhanced communication:** Language barriers will fade as machines become adept at translating languages flawlessly, bridging cultures and facilitating global communication.
- **Seamless interactions:** Natural language interfaces will enable you to interact with computers and devices using your voice or text, making technology more accessible and intuitive.

However, this future also raises critical questions about the ethical use of NLP. We need to address issues like bias in algorithms, the potential misuse of NLP for malicious purposes, and the impact on privacy and security.

As we continue to develop NLP, it's crucial to ensure that these technologies are used responsibly and ethically, contributing to a more informed, connected, and equitable world. NLP has the potential to revolutionize how we communicate and interact with technology, but it's up to us to shape its future for the greater good.

Tokenization and Representation

Before machines can understand and process human language, we need a way to bridge the gap between text, which is inherently symbolic and abstract, and the numerical data that computers excel at manipulating. This is where the magic of tokenization and word embeddings comes in.

Imagine a child learning to read. Initially, they see words as a collection of squiggly lines. Over time, they learn to recognize individual letters, then combine them into meaningful words, and finally, comprehend sentences and paragraphs. Computers, in a way, go through a similar process. They begin by breaking down text into its fundamental building blocks – individual words or units called tokens.

Tokenization is the process of dividing a text into a sequence of tokens. These tokens can be words, punctuation marks, or even individual characters, depending on the specific task. For example, the sentence "The quick brown fox jumps over the lazy dog" can be tokenized into the following sequence:

```['The', 'quick', 'brown', 'fox', 'jumps', 'over', 'the', 'lazy', 'dog']```

This sequence of tokens represents the underlying structure of the sentence, making it easier for computers to process. However, simply tokenizing the text doesn't tell us much about the meaning or relationships between words. To truly understand language, computers need to learn how words relate to each other and their overall context. This is where word embeddings come into play.

Word embeddings are numerical representations of words that capture their semantic meaning and relationships. They essentially translate words into a mathematical space where similar words are closer together, while dissimilar words are farther apart. Think of it as a map where each word is a point, and the proximity of points indicates the similarity of their meanings.

There are various techniques for creating word embeddings, but a popular method is word2vec, which uses a neural network to learn word representations from a large corpus of text. The network analyzes the contexts in which words appear, identi-
```

fying patterns and relationships. For instance, words like "king," "queen," and "prince" will be clustered together in the embedding space, reflecting their shared royal connotations.

Word embeddings are powerful tools for a variety of NLP tasks, including:

- **Text similarity:** By comparing the distances between word embeddings, computers can determine how similar two pieces of text are.
- **Sentiment analysis:** Embeddings can help identify the emotional tone of the text, whether it's positive, negative, or neutral.
- **Machine translation:** Word embeddings can aid in translating languages by capturing the semantic meaning of words and facilitating their mapping to equivalent words in another language.

Here's an example of how word embeddings can be used to solve a practical problem. Imagine you have a large dataset of customer reviews for a product. You want to analyze these reviews to understand the overall sentiment towards the product.

Using word embeddings, you can represent each review as a vector (a mathematical representation of points in space), where the coordinates of the vector correspond to the embeddings of the words in the review. By calculating the average embedding of all the words in a review, you can obtain a single vector that represents the sentiment of the review.

This way, you can cluster reviews based on their average embeddings, identifying positive, negative, or neutral sentiment groups. This allows you to analyze the sentiment of the entire dataset efficiently and understand which aspects of the product are generating positive or negative feedback.

Word embeddings are a crucial component of modern NLP systems, allowing machines to understand the nuances of human language. They have enabled significant advancements in various fields, from automated customer service to personalized recommendations and even medical diagnostics. As AI research continues to advance, we can expect even more sophisticated and powerful word embedding techniques to emerge, further enhancing the capabilities of machines to comprehend and interact with the complexities of human language.

Capturing the Essence of Language

Language models are the heart of natural language processing (NLP), providing machines with the ability to understand the nuances of human communication. They act as the bridge between raw text and the complex world of meaning, enabling computers to decipher the patterns and structures hidden within language.

Imagine a language model as a sophisticated detective, meticulously piecing together clues from a vast corpus of text. This corpus could be anything from a collection of books to a massive dataset of social media posts. Just as a detective analyzes fingerprints and footprints, the language model identifies the statistical patterns and relationships between words. These patterns reveal the underlying structure of language, allowing the model to predict the next word in a sequence, generate coherent text, and even translate between languages.

There are two main categories of language models: statistical language models and neural language models.

Statistical Language Models: The Foundations of Language Understanding

Statistical language models emerged as the pioneers in the field of language modeling. These models, rooted in the principles of probability and statistics, rely on analyzing vast amounts of text to identify the likelihood of words appearing together.

One of the earliest and most influential statistical language models is the n-gram model. This model calculates the probability of a word appearing in a sequence based on the preceding n-1 words. For instance, a bigram model considers the probability of a word given the previous word. This model helps us understand the likelihood of "the" following "cat," which is much higher than "the" following "zebra."

While n-gram models proved effective in many applications, they suffer from limitations. They are unable to capture long-range dependencies in language, struggle with rare words, and require significant computational resources to train.

Neural Language Models: The Rise of Deep Learning in Language

Neural language models, powered by deep learning, have revolutionized the field of language modeling. They leverage the power of artificial neural networks, inspired by the structure and function of the human brain, to learn intricate representations of language.

These models learn to represent words as vectors in a high-dimensional space, capturing semantic relationships between words. For instance, the vectors for "king" and "queen" might be closer together than the vectors for "king" and "apple," reflecting their semantic similarity.

One of the most impactful neural language models is the recurrent neural network (RNN), specifically the long short-term memory (LSTM) variant. RNNs excel in capturing long-range dependencies in text, allowing them to understand context and maintain information across long sequences. This is crucial for tasks like machine translation, where the meaning of a word can be influenced by words appearing much earlier in the sentence.

Transformative Applications of Language Models

The rise of language models has ushered in a new era of language-based AI applications, transforming fields like:

- **Machine Translation:** Language models power state-of-the-art machine translation systems, bridging the gap between languages and fostering global communication.
- **Text Summarization:** They help condense lengthy documents into concise summaries, allowing us to quickly grasp the essential information.
- **Sentiment Analysis:** By analyzing the emotional tone of text, language models enable businesses to understand customer opinions and gauge public sentiment.
- **Chatbots:** Language models are the driving force behind sophisticated chatbots, enabling natural and engaging conversations with machines.

The Future of Language Models: A Journey of Continuous Evolution

Language models are not just a technological marvel, but a testament to our understanding of language itself. As these models continue to evolve, they are paving the way for increasingly sophisticated and human-like interactions with machines.

Here are some exciting advancements to expect in the future of language models:

- **Multimodal Language Models:** Integrating visual, auditory, and other sensory information into language models will enable machines to understand and generate a richer representation of the world.
- **Contextualized Language Models:** Models that can dynamically adapt to the context of a conversation, taking into account previous interactions and knowledge, will lead to a more natural and engaging dialogue.
- **Explainable Language Models:** As language models become more complex, it is crucial to develop methods for explaining their decisions and making their internal workings more transparent.

The future of language models holds immense potential, promising to revolutionize how we communicate, learn, and interact with the world around us. As these models continue to evolve, we can expect an era where machines truly understand and respond to language in a way that was once thought to be exclusive to humans.

From Machine to Chatbots

Imagine a world where computers can understand and respond to human language as naturally as we do. This is the realm of Natural Language Processing (NLP), a branch of AI that empowers machines to comprehend, interpret, and generate human language.

NLP has become a transformative force in various fields, revolutionizing how we interact with technology and information. It's the magic behind everything from translating languages effortlessly to engaging in conversations with intelligent chatbots. Let's delve into the fascinating world of NLP and uncover its diverse applications.

Machine Translation: Breaking Down Language Barriers

Remember those clunky translation programs of the past, struggling to convey meaning accurately? NLP has revolutionized machine translation, enabling computers to translate languages with remarkable fluency and precision. This technology has bridged communication gaps across the globe, enabling individuals to access information, share ideas, and collaborate in different languages.

At the heart of machine translation lies the power of statistical and neural language models. These models learn the intricacies of language by analyzing massive datasets of text and code. By uncovering the statistical patterns and relationships between words, they can translate sentences with an astonishing level of accuracy.

Take, for instance, Google Translate. Powered by advanced neural networks, it has become an indispensable tool for millions of users worldwide. It can translate between dozens of languages, providing real-time translations for websites, documents, and even spoken language. This technology has broken down linguistic barriers, fostering global communication and understanding.

Sentiment Analysis: Unlocking Emotions in Text

Have you ever wondered about the emotions behind a tweet or a product review? Sentiment analysis, a powerful NLP application, allows us to analyze text and extract the underlying sentiment—whether it's positive, negative, or neutral. It enables us to gauge public opinion, understand customer feedback, and even monitor brand reputation.

Sentiment analysis is particularly useful in social media monitoring. By analyzing large volumes of social media posts, businesses can gain valuable insights into customer sentiment towards their products or services. They can track trends, identify potential issues, and respond proactively to customer feedback.

Beyond social media, sentiment analysis is also employed in market research, financial analysis, and political forecasting. It helps businesses make data-driven decisions, understand public opinion, and predict future trends.

Text Summarization: Condensing Information into Concise Summaries

In an era of information overload, text summarization has emerged as a vital tool for distilling large amounts of information into concise and meaningful summaries. NLP-powered summarizers can scan lengthy articles, reports, and documents, identifying the key points and presenting them in a condensed format.

Imagine a world where you can quickly grasp the essence of a long research paper or understand the key takeaways from a complex news report. NLP-powered summarizers make this possible, saving valuable time and effort.

These technologies are employed in various settings, from news aggregation websites that provide brief overviews of breaking news stories to research databases that generate summaries of scientific articles. Text summarization also plays a crucial role in education, enabling students to quickly grasp the key concepts in textbooks and articles.

Chatbot Development: Creating Conversational AI Agents

Chatbots, the AI-powered conversational agents, have become ubiquitous in our digital lives. From customer service websites to social media platforms, they are transforming how we interact with businesses and services. Chatbots powered by NLP can understand and respond to natural language, providing personalized and efficient assistance.

These AI agents are designed to simulate human conversation, understanding intent, responding to questions, and providing relevant information. They are particularly useful in customer service, where they can handle routine inquiries, provide support, and even complete transactions.

The rise of conversational AI has ushered in a new era of human-computer interaction, making technology more accessible, efficient, and engaging. Chatbots are continually evolving, becoming more sophisticated and capable of handling increasingly complex conversations.

The Future of NLP: Unveiling New Possibilities

NLP is a constantly evolving field, driven by advancements in deep learning, natural language understanding, and artificial intelligence. The future of NLP holds tremendous potential for revolutionizing various aspects of our lives.

Imagine a world where AI assistants can understand our needs and desires, anticipate our questions, and provide personalized solutions. NLP will power the next generation of AI assistants, enabling seamless and intuitive interactions with machines.

Moreover, NLP is poised to play a critical role in the development of personalized learning experiences, where AI tutors can tailor education to individual learning styles and needs. NLP will also enable the creation of more immersive and engaging virtual worlds, allowing us to interact with digital environments and characters in a more natural and intuitive way.

As we navigate this exciting era of AI, NLP will continue to push the boundaries of human-computer interaction, empowering us to communicate, learn, and create in new and innovative ways. The future of NLP is full of possibilities, shaping a world where technology seamlessly complements and enhances our human capabilities.

Conversational AI and Beyond

The realm of Natural Language Processing (NLP) is poised for a future brimming with exciting possibilities, pushing the boundaries of human-machine interaction. As NLP matures, it's primed to become a driving force behind the development of conversational AI, transforming the way we interact with technology. Imagine a world where you can effortlessly converse with your devices, seamlessly asking questions, expressing desires, and receiving insightful responses. This vision is not merely science fiction; it's the imminent reality of conversational AI.

Imagine a world where your virtual assistant anticipates your needs before you even articulate them. A world where you can engage in natural, fluid conversations with your smartphone, your car, or even your refrigerator. Conversational AI, powered by the advancements in NLP, is paving the way for this future.

At the heart of conversational AI lies the ability to understand and respond to human language in a way that feels natural and intuitive. It's no longer about rigid commands and pre-programmed responses; it's about engaging in nuanced dialogues, understanding context, and adapting to individual preferences.

This transformative potential stems from several key developments in NLP:

- **Enhanced Language Models:** The emergence of sophisticated language models, such as BERT, GPT-3, and LaMDA, has dramatically improved the ability of AI systems to understand and generate human-like text. These models are trained on massive datasets of text, allowing them to grasp complex nuances of language, including context, sentiment, and intent.
- **Contextual Understanding:** Conversational AI systems are now able to maintain context throughout a conversation, remembering previous turns and using that information to generate more relevant and coherent responses. This means that interactions feel

more natural and engaging, as if you're having a genuine dialogue with another human.

- **Personalization and Adaptability:** With the help of NLP, conversational AI systems can learn and adapt to individual preferences, tailoring their responses and interactions to suit each user. This personalized experience creates a more intimate and valuable relationship between humans and machines.

The Rise of Conversational AI

Conversational AI is rapidly permeating various aspects of our lives, revolutionizing how we interact with technology. Here are some prominent examples:

- **Chatbots and Virtual Assistants:** Chatbots are becoming increasingly sophisticated, able to handle complex customer inquiries, provide personalized recommendations, and assist with various tasks. Virtual assistants, such as Siri, Alexa, and Google Assistant, are evolving to become more conversational, capable of understanding and responding to a wide range of requests and questions.
- **Customer Service and Support:** Conversational AI is transforming customer service by automating routine tasks, resolving inquiries quickly, and providing 24/7 support. This reduces wait times, increases customer satisfaction, and allows human agents to focus on more complex issues.
- **Education and Training:** Conversational AI is finding its way into classrooms, offering personalized learning experiences, providing instant feedback, and

assisting students with their queries. It's also being used to create interactive training programs for employees, offering a more engaging and effective learning experience.

- **Healthcare:** Conversational AI is being used to provide healthcare information, schedule appointments, remind patients about medications, and even assist with diagnosis and treatment. The potential for conversational AI to improve healthcare access and outcomes is immense.

Beyond Conversational AI

The future of NLP extends far beyond conversational AI. The field is actively exploring new frontiers, driven by an insatiable hunger to empower machines with a deeper understanding of human language. Here are some exciting areas where NLP is poised to make a significant impact:

- **Automatic Text Generation:** NLP is driving advancements in automatic text generation, enabling machines to write articles, summaries, creative content, and even code. This has the potential to revolutionize content creation, freeing up human writers to focus on more creative and strategic tasks.
- **Sentiment Analysis and Opinion Mining:** NLP is being used to analyze and understand sentiment expressed in text, allowing businesses to gain insights into customer opinions, public perception, and market trends. This information is invaluable for making informed decisions and improving products and services.

- **Machine Translation:** NLP is constantly pushing the boundaries of machine translation, enabling more accurate and nuanced translations across languages. This has the potential to break down communication barriers and foster a more interconnected world.
- **Text Summarization:** NLP is being used to generate concise summaries of lengthy texts, allowing people to quickly grasp the essence of information without having to read through entire documents. This has applications in news reporting, research, and education.
- **Information Extraction and Knowledge Graph Construction:** NLP is enabling machines to extract structured information from unstructured text, such as news articles, reports, and scientific papers. This information can be used to build knowledge graphs, which represent relationships and connections between entities, facilitating complex knowledge discovery and reasoning.

The Ethical Landscape of NLP

While NLP's potential is vast, it's essential to acknowledge the ethical considerations that accompany its advancement. As NLP systems become more sophisticated, they raise concerns about:

- **Bias and Fairness:** NLP models are trained on data that reflects societal biases, potentially leading to discriminatory outcomes. It's crucial to develop algorithms that mitigate bias and ensure fairness in their applications.

- **Privacy and Security:** NLP applications often involve processing sensitive personal data, raising concerns about privacy violations and security breaches. Robust safeguards and regulations are necessary to protect individual privacy and ensure the secure handling of data.
- **Job Displacement:** The automation capabilities of NLP raise concerns about potential job displacement in fields that rely heavily on human language processing, such as writing, translation, and customer service. It's important to consider the societal implications of these advancements and explore strategies for reskilling and retraining the workforce.

The Future is Conversational:

The future of NLP is bright and filled with promise, with conversational AI at the forefront. As language models continue to evolve, and our understanding of language deepens, we can expect to see increasingly natural and intuitive interactions between humans and machines. From chatbots that understand our emotions to AI-powered systems that learn and adapt to our individual needs, the future holds a world where language becomes a seamless bridge between humans and technology.

But with this advancement comes the responsibility to ensure that NLP is developed and used ethically, safeguarding our privacy, mitigating bias, and ensuring that AI serves humanity. The future of NLP is not just about technological progress; it's about shaping a future where technology enhances our lives, empowering us to communicate, learn, and collaborate in new and exciting ways.

As we journey into this future, it's vital to remember that NLP is a tool, and like any tool, it can be used for good or for harm. It's our collective responsibility to ensure that we harness the power of NLP for positive impact, creating a future where language is a force for connection, understanding, and progress.

Chapter 5

Computer Vision

Giving Machines the Power of Sight

A Source of Inspiration for Computer Vision

The human visual system is a marvel of biological engineering, an intricate network of specialized cells and pathways that enable us to perceive the world around us. It's a testament to the power of evolution, sculpted over millions of years to extract meaningful information from the vast sea of visual stimuli.

At its core, our visual system operates through a complex interplay of light, optics, and neural processing. Light enters the eye through the cornea, a transparent outer layer that focuses the incoming light. It then passes through the pupil, an adjustable opening that controls the amount of light entering the eye. The lens, a flexible structure behind the pupil, further refines the light, focusing it onto the retina, a light-sensitive layer lining the back of the eye.

The retina itself is a complex tapestry of specialized cells, including photoreceptor cells called rods and cones, which convert light into electrical signals. Rods are responsible for vision in low-light conditions, while cones are responsible for color vision. These signals are then transmitted through a network of neurons to the brain, where they are processed and interpreted.

The brain then reconstructs a representation of the world based on these electrical signals, taking into account factors like shape, color, depth, and motion. This process, known as visual perception, allows us to understand the world around us, navigate our surroundings, and engage in complex visual tasks.

The remarkable capabilities of the human visual system have long been a source of inspiration for researchers seeking to imbue machines with the power of sight. Computer vision, a field of artificial intelligence that aims to give computers the ability to "see" and interpret images and videos, has been profoundly influenced by our understanding of the human visual system.

Early computer vision systems were often inspired by the workings of the eye, attempting to mimic the processes of light detection, image formation, and feature extraction. However, as the field progressed, researchers began to explore more sophisticated computational models, drawing inspiration not only from the structure of the eye but also from the complex neural processes involved in visual perception.

This led to the development of artificial neural networks, computational models inspired by the structure and function of the human brain. Artificial neural networks consist of interconnected nodes, or neurons, which process and transmit information. Just as neurons in the brain learn to recognize patterns by adjusting the strength of their connections, artificial neurons learn by adjusting the weights of their connections, adapting to new data and improving their ability to recognize patterns.

This ability to learn from data has been central to the success of deep learning, a subfield of machine learning that uses deep artificial neural networks to extract complex features from raw data. Deep learning algorithms have revolutionized computer vision, enabling machines to perform tasks such as object recognition, image classification, and image segmentation with unprecedented accuracy.

One of the key insights gleaned from the human visual system that has shaped computer vision research is the concept of hierarchical feature extraction. Our brains process visual information in a hierarchical manner, starting with simple features like edges and lines and gradually building up to more complex features like objects and scenes.

Deep learning models, inspired by this hierarchical structure, process images in a similar way, starting with convolutional layers that extract low-level features, followed by subsequent layers that learn increasingly complex features. This hierarchical approach allows deep learning models to extract rich and meaningful information from images, enabling them to achieve high levels of accuracy in various computer vision tasks.

Another crucial aspect of the human visual system that has inspired computer vision research is the concept of attention. Our brains are constantly bombarded with visual information, but we only pay attention to a small subset of it. Attention mechanisms help us focus on the most relevant information, filtering out irrelevant details and enabling us to efficiently process complex visual scenes.

Computer vision researchers have developed similar attention mechanisms for deep learning models, allowing them to selectively focus on the most informative parts of an image, improving their performance in tasks such as object detection and image segmentation.

The inspiration drawn from the human visual system has played a crucial role in advancing computer vision, leading to significant breakthroughs in image recognition, object detection, and scene understanding. However, despite these advancements, computer vision still faces challenges that the human visual system tackles effortlessly.

For example, humans can easily perceive depth and motion, tasks that are still difficult for machines. Moreover, the human visual system is highly adaptable, capable of learning new visual concepts and adjusting to changing environments. Computer vision systems, while becoming increasingly sophisticated, still lag behind human performance in terms of adaptability and generalizability.

The future of computer vision lies in continuing to draw inspiration from the human visual system, striving to develop systems that can match or even surpass human capabilities. This will involve exploring new computational models, developing more robust and adaptable learning algorithms, and leveraging the power of artificial intelligence to push the boundaries of what machines can see and understand.

The journey towards giving machines the power of sight is a fascinating one, a testament to the human desire to understand and replicate the wonders of our natural world. By drawing inspiration from the human visual system, researchers are making strides in unlocking the potential of computer vision, transforming the way we interact with the world around us.

Extracting Informaion from Pixels

Imagine a world where computers can understand and interpret images just like humans do. This is the realm of computer vision, a field of AI that's revolutionizing how we interact with the world around us.

At the heart of computer vision lies image processing – the art of teaching machines to "see" and make sense of the visual world. It's like giving computers a pair of eyes, allowing them to analyze and manipulate digital images in ways that were once unimaginable.

Think of a photo you take with your phone. It's just a collection of pixels, tiny squares of color arranged in a grid. To a human, those pixels tell a story, revealing objects, textures, and emotions. But for a computer, those pixels are just numbers.

Image processing is the bridge that connects these two worlds. It's the process of extracting meaningful information from those raw pixels, allowing computers to understand the content of an image and respond accordingly.

Unveiling the Secrets Within Pixels

The journey of image processing begins with analyzing individual pixels. Computers can examine the color, brightness, and position of each pixel, uncovering hidden patterns and relationships.

For example, imagine a picture of a sunset. To a human, the gradient of colors, the soft glow, and the hazy horizon evoke a sense of tranquility. To a computer, it's just a collection of pixels, each with a specific color value.

Image processing allows computers to analyze the arrangement of colors, identify the gradual change from bright orange to deep purple, and recognize the characteristic features of a sunset. This analysis goes beyond just recognizing the image as a "sunset," it allows the computer to understand the mood, the time of day, and even the location.

Beyond Simple Recognition

Image processing isn't limited to just recognizing objects. It encompasses a wide range of techniques that allow computers to manipulate and enhance images in various ways.

1. **Image Enhancement:** Imagine a blurry photo that you want to sharpen. Image processing algorithms can analyze the pixels and adjust their brightness, contrast, and sharpness, making the image clearer and more detailed.
2. **Noise Reduction:** Ever taken a photo in low light and noticed the grainy noise? Image processing can help by analyzing the noise patterns and smoothing out the image, reducing the distracting graininess.
3. **Image Segmentation:** Imagine wanting to separate the foreground from the background in an image. Image processing techniques can identify the boundaries between objects and the background, allowing you to extract specific parts of the image or even create a digital cutout.
4. **Object Detection:** This is where things start getting really interesting. Image processing allows computers

to identify specific objects within an image, like cars, faces, or animals. This is the foundation for self-driving cars, facial recognition systems, and even medical imaging analysis.

5. **Image Restoration:** Imagine an old, faded photograph that you want to restore. Image processing can analyze the damage, fill in missing pixels, and adjust colors to bring the image back to life.

The Power of Algorithms

Behind these image processing techniques lies a fascinating world of algorithms. These are sets of instructions that computers follow to analyze and manipulate images.

Some algorithms are designed to enhance image quality, while others are specifically tailored to identify certain objects or features. Each algorithm relies on specific mathematical operations to manipulate the pixels, extracting hidden information and transforming the image.

The Evolution of Image Processing

Image processing has come a long way from simple pixel manipulation. With the advent of machine learning and deep learning, computers are now able to learn from vast amounts of data, becoming even more sophisticated in their ability to understand and interpret images.

Deep learning algorithms, particularly convolutional neural networks (CNNs), have proven to be incredibly powerful for image recognition tasks. These networks mimic the structure of the human brain, allowing computers to learn complex patterns and relationships from images, much like humans do.

Applications Across Industries

Image processing is no longer confined to the realm of research. It's permeating various industries, transforming the way we live, work, and interact with the world.

1. **Healthcare:** Medical imaging plays a crucial role in diagnosis and treatment. Image processing is used to analyze X-rays, MRIs, and CT scans, helping doctors identify tumors, fractures, and other abnormalities. This technology is revolutionizing medical diagnosis, leading to earlier detection and more effective treatment.
2. **Security:** Facial recognition systems are increasingly common, used for security purposes at airports, banks, and even in our smartphones. Image processing algorithms analyze facial features, matching them to databases and helping identify individuals.
3. **Self-Driving Cars:** Self-driving cars rely heavily on image processing. Cameras mounted on the vehicles capture images of the road, which are then analyzed by algorithms to identify other vehicles, pedestrians, traffic signs, and obstacles. This information enables the car to navigate safely and autonomously.
4. **Retail:** Image processing is used in retail for various purposes, such as inventory management, customer behavior analysis, and even personalized shopping recommendations. By analyzing images of store shelves, computers can monitor stock levels and identify potential shortages.

The Future of Image Processing

Image processing continues to evolve, with advancements in deep learning, computer vision, and sensor technology. The future holds exciting possibilities, with computers becoming even more adept at understanding and interpreting images.

We can expect to see

1. **Improved Image Quality:** Algorithms will become more sophisticated at reducing noise, enhancing sharpness, and restoring faded images, creating even more realistic and high-quality visuals.
2. **Advanced Object Recognition:** Computers will be able to recognize objects with greater accuracy and detail, even in complex scenes and challenging environments.
3. **Enhanced Image Understanding:** Image processing will go beyond simple object recognition, allowing computers to understand the context and meaning behind images, interpreting scenes, emotions, and even narratives.
4. **Integration with Other Technologies:** Image processing will be seamlessly integrated with other technologies, such as augmented reality and virtual reality, creating immersive and interactive experiences.

The world of image processing is brimming with possibilities, shaping the way we interact with the visual world and opening up new frontiers in technology, healthcare, security, and countless other industries. As computer vision continues to evolve, we can expect to see even more innovative applications that will transform our lives and the world around us.

THE POWERHOUSE OF IMAGE RECOGNITION

Convolutional neural networks (CNNs) are a groundbreaking type of artificial neural network specifically designed for processing and analyzing visual information. They have become the cornerstone of modern computer vision, powering a wide range of applications from facial recognition to medical image analysis.

Imagine a computer that can see and understand the world around it, just like humans do. That's the goal of computer vision, and CNNs are at the heart of this revolution. These networks are inspired by the structure and function of the human visual cortex, where information is processed in a hierarchical and layered fashion.

The Core of CNNs: Convolutional Layers

The secret to CNNs' success lies in their convolutional layers. These layers are designed to extract features from images by performing a series of mathematical operations. The process is analogous to how humans scan images, focusing on specific regions and detecting patterns like edges, shapes, and textures.

Think of it like using a magnifying glass to examine a picture. Each convolutional layer acts like a specialized magnifying glass, searching for specific patterns within the image. These patterns, or features, are then passed on to subsequent layers, where they are further analyzed and combined to form higher-level representations.

Image Classification: Recognizing What's in a Picture

One of the most common applications of CNNs is image classification. This involves training a CNN to identify the objects or scenes depicted in an image. For example, a CNN can be trained to distinguish between images of cats and dogs, or to classify images of different types of flowers.

The process begins by feeding a CNN thousands of labeled images. Each image is associated with a specific class, such as "cat" or "dog." The CNN then analyzes these images, learning to recognize patterns that are unique to each class.

During training, the CNN's convolutional layers gradually extract features from the images. As the network progresses through the layers, the features become more abstract and complex, representing higher-level concepts like the presence of a tail or the texture of fur.

Once the CNN is trained, it can be used to classify new images. When presented with an unseen image, the CNN extracts features from it, just as it did during training. It then compares these features to those it learned during training, predicting the most likely class for the image.

Object Detection: Identifying and Locating Objects in Images

While image classification tells us what's in a picture, object detection takes it a step further by identifying and locating specific objects within the image. This capability has immense practical applications, such as self-driving cars identifying other vehicles and pedestrians, or security systems detecting suspicious objects in surveillance footage.

Object detection CNNs employ additional layers beyond the convolutional layers, specifically, "region proposal" and "bounding box" layers. These layers aim to pinpoint the exact location and size of the detected objects within the image.

Think of it as a treasure hunt within an image. The convolutional layers are like the explorers, seeking out interesting features. The region proposal layers act as the map makers, identifying potential locations for hidden treasures. Finally, the bounding box layers draw the treasure chests, outlining the precise location of the detected objects.

Image Segmentation: Dividing an Image into Meaningful Regions

Image segmentation is a crucial task in computer vision, where the goal is to divide an image into distinct regions based on their characteristics. This allows computers to understand not just the objects in an image, but also their relationships and spatial arrangement.

CNNs are particularly effective for image segmentation because they can learn to identify complex relationships between pixels. Instead of just recognizing objects, they can segment an image into meaningful parts, such as foreground and background, or even different parts of the same object.

An Example: Recognizing and Segmenting a Dog

Let's imagine a CNN being used to analyze a photo of a dog. The convolutional layers would initially detect basic features like edges, shapes, and textures. As the network progresses, these features would be combined and analyzed to recognize higher-level patterns specific to a dog, such as a tail, four legs, and fur.

To perform object detection, additional layers would pinpoint the exact location of the dog within the image, drawing a bounding box around its outline. For image segmentation, the CNN would go further, dividing the image into regions representing the dog's body, its tail, its legs, and its fur.

Beyond Image Recognition: Expanding the Power of CNNs

While image recognition remains a core application of CNNs, these networks have proven their versatility in other fields as well. They are increasingly being used for:

- **Medical Imaging:** CNNs are helping to automate the analysis of medical images, such as X-rays, MRIs, and CT scans, leading to faster and more accurate diagnoses.
- **Video Analysis:** CNNs can analyze videos, tracking objects over time, recognizing actions, and even detecting emotions.
- **Text Recognition:** CNNs are being used to recognize text in images, such as handwritten notes, scanned documents, and street signs.
- **Audio Processing:** CNNs are even finding applications in audio processing, where they can analyze sound signals to identify speech, music, and other sounds.

The Future of CNNs: Towards a Deeper Understanding

The development of CNNs has revolutionized computer vision, enabling machines to "see" and interpret the world in ways that were previously unimaginable. As research continues, CNNs are becoming increasingly sophisticated, capable of understanding and responding to complex visual information.

Future advancements in CNN architecture, training methods, and data availability will likely lead to even more remarkable achievements. These advancements may include:

- **Improved Object Detection and Recognition:** CNNs will become more accurate and robust at identifying objects, even in challenging conditions, such as low-light or cluttered environments.
- **Advanced Image Segmentation:** CNNs will be able to segment images with greater precision and detail, unlocking new possibilities for understanding complex scenes and objects.
- **Depth Perception and Scene Understanding:** CNNs will gain the ability to understand the three-dimensional structure of scenes, allowing them to perceive depth, navigate environments, and interact with objects more naturally.
- **Human-Computer Interaction:** CNNs will play a crucial role in developing intuitive and natural forms of human-computer interaction, such as gesture recognition, facial expression analysis, and eye tracking.

CNNs are not just a technological marvel, they are a powerful tool for understanding and interacting with the world. As they continue to evolve, they have the potential to unlock unprecedented possibilities in fields ranging from healthcare and transportation to entertainment and beyond.

From Self-Driving Cars to Medical Diagnosis

5.4 Applications of Computer Vision: From Self-Driving Cars to Medical Diagnosis

Computer vision, having learned to "see" and interpret the world, has blossomed into an indispensable tool across a vast spectrum of industries. Let's embark on a journey through the diverse realms where computer vision is making a tangible impact:

1. Autonomous Vehicles: The Road to Driverless Cars

Imagine a world where cars navigate roads without human intervention, seamlessly adjusting to traffic, road conditions, and unforeseen obstacles. This vision of autonomous vehicles is no longer a distant dream, thanks to the remarkable strides made in computer vision.

At the heart of self-driving cars lies a sophisticated system of sensors, including cameras, LiDAR (Light Detection and Ranging), and radar, working in concert to capture a 360-degree view of the surroundings. Computer vision algorithms then analyze this data, identifying objects like cars, pedestrians, traffic lights, and road signs, and predicting their movements. This information empowers the vehicle to make informed decisions, steering, accelerating, and braking with precision.

The applications of self-driving cars extend beyond personal transportation. They hold the promise of revolutionizing logistics, transforming freight delivery, and even reshaping urban planning. Imagine a world where trucks navigate highways autonomously, reducing the risk of accidents, optimizing delivery routes, and freeing up human drivers for other tasks. This vision of autonomous transportation is poised to reshape the way we move around our cities and the world.

2. Facial Recognition: Unveiling Identities in a Blink of an Eye

Facial recognition, a cornerstone of computer vision, empowers machines to identify individuals based on their unique facial features. This technology has revolutionized security, unlocking doors, verifying identities, and even tracking individuals in public spaces.

The process of facial recognition involves capturing a live image or a still photograph and comparing it to a database of known faces. Advanced algorithms analyze facial features, including the distance between eyes, the shape of the nose, and the contours of the chin, to determine a match.

While facial recognition holds immense potential for security and convenience, it has also sparked ethical debates about privacy and potential misuse. Concerns have been raised about the potential for mass surveillance, the possibility of false positives, and the potential for discrimination based on facial features.

The responsible deployment of facial recognition technology requires careful consideration of these ethical implications. Developing transparent and accountable systems, ensuring accuracy, and protecting individual rights are crucial to harnessing the power of this technology for good.

3. Medical Imaging Analysis: Enhancing Diagnosis and Treatment

In the realm of healthcare, computer vision has emerged as a powerful tool for enhancing medical diagnosis and treatment. By analyzing medical images, such as X-rays, CT scans, and MRIs, computer vision algorithms can identify abnormalities, detect early signs of disease, and assist in the development of personalized treatment plans.

One notable application is in the diagnosis of cancer. Computer vision algorithms can analyze mammograms to detect early signs of breast cancer, enabling timely intervention and improving patient outcomes. Similarly, these algorithms can assist in identifying cancerous tumors in lung X-rays and detecting anomalies in brain MRIs.

Beyond diagnosis, computer vision is transforming surgical procedures, assisting surgeons with real-time guidance during complex operations, and aiding in the development of minimally invasive techniques. These advancements are ushering in a new era of precision and effectiveness in the healthcare field.

4. Visual Search: Finding What You See

Imagine a world where you can simply point your smartphone camera at an object and instantly find relevant information about it. Visual search engines, powered by computer vision, are making this vision a reality.

Visual search engines analyze images, extracting key features and patterns, and then comparing them to a vast database of images and information. This allows users to search for products, landmarks, artworks, or even recipes based on images they capture.

The applications of visual search extend beyond simple image recognition. It is being used to enhance online shopping experiences, helping users find similar products or discover new items based on their visual preferences. It is also being used in fashion, allowing users to find similar clothing items based on images of outfits they see.

As computer vision technology continues to evolve, we can expect even more innovative and intuitive visual search applications to emerge, transforming the way we interact with the world around us.

5. Object Detection: Seeing the World in Detail

Object detection, a fundamental task in computer vision, involves identifying and localizing objects within images or videos. This technology powers applications ranging from self-driving cars to security systems to retail analytics.

Object detection algorithms are trained on vast datasets of labeled images, enabling them to recognize objects like cars, pedestrians, bicycles, traffic lights, and other relevant entities. These algorithms can also distinguish between different types of objects, such as different car models or specific breeds of dogs.

The applications of object detection are wide-ranging. In self-driving cars, it is used to detect obstacles and make safe navigation decisions. In security systems, it is used to identify suspicious activities and trigger alerts. In retail analytics, it is used to track customer behavior and optimize store layout.

6. Image Segmentation: Dividing and Conquer

Image segmentation, a key aspect of computer vision, involves partitioning an image into meaningful regions, identifying different objects or areas of interest. This technology finds applications in diverse fields, from medical imaging to autonomous driving to video editing.

In medical imaging, image segmentation is used to identify tumors, organs, and other structures, aiding in diagnosis, surgical planning, and treatment monitoring. In autonomous driving, it is used to separate the road from obstacles, enabling accurate navigation and obstacle avoidance. In video editing, it is used to isolate specific objects or regions of interest, allowing for creative manipulations and special effects.

7. Sports Analytics: The Next Level of Game Analysis

Sports, a realm of athletic prowess and strategic brilliance, is undergoing a transformation with the integration of computer vision. By analyzing video footage of games, computer vision algorithms can track player movements, predict ball trajectories, and even detect potential violations of rules.

This technology is revolutionizing sports analysis, providing coaches with valuable insights into player performance, team strategy, and game dynamics. It also enhances the viewing experience for fans, offering real-time statistics, player tracking, and augmented reality overlays.

8. Security and Surveillance: A New Age of Vigilance

Computer vision is playing a crucial role in enhancing security and surveillance, providing a powerful tool for identifying potential threats, monitoring activities, and responding to incidents.

Security systems equipped with computer vision can detect suspicious activity, track individuals in real time, and identify potential threats based on learned patterns of behavior. These systems can also be used for facial recognition, access control, and intrusion detection.

9. Agriculture: Optimizing Crops and Yield

Agriculture, the backbone of food production, is benefiting from the transformative power of computer vision. By analyzing images and videos of crops, computer vision algorithms can monitor plant health, detect diseases and pests, and optimize irrigation and fertilization.

This technology is helping farmers to improve crop yields, reduce waste, and make more efficient use of resources. It is also aiding in the development of precision agriculture practices, where data-driven insights guide every step of the farming process.

10. Manufacturing: Optimizing Production and Quality Control

In manufacturing, computer vision is enhancing production processes, improving quality control, and boosting efficiency. Cameras and sensors integrated into production lines can monitor the assembly process, detect defects, and ensure product quality.

This technology is also being used for robotics, enabling robots to perform complex tasks, such as picking and placing objects, with accuracy and precision. Computer vision is transforming manufacturing, paving the way for more efficient and automated production lines.

The Future of Computer Vision: A Vision of Possibilities

Computer vision, having already revolutionized numerous fields, is poised for even greater advancements in the years to come. As research progresses and computational power increases, we can anticipate breakthroughs in areas like:

- **Depth Perception:** Enabling machines to perceive the world in 3D, allowing for more accurate navigation, object recognition, and scene understanding.
- **Scene Understanding:** Teaching machines to interpret complex scenes, understanding the relationships between objects and their context.

- **Human-Computer Interaction:** Creating more intuitive and natural interactions between humans and machines, using gestures, facial expressions, and gaze tracking.
- **Medical Imaging:** Developing more sophisticated algorithms for medical image analysis, improving diagnosis, treatment planning, and personalized medicine.

The future of computer vision is brimming with possibilities, promising to reshape our world in ways we can only begin to imagine. As this technology continues to evolve, it has the potential to enhance our lives, improve our health, and solve some of the world's most pressing challenges.

Building on the Foundations

The future of computer vision is brimming with possibilities, poised to revolutionize how we interact with the world and each other. We are on the cusp of a new era where machines will not only see but also understand and interpret the visual world with an unprecedented level of sophistication.

One exciting frontier is the pursuit of depth perception, enabling machines to perceive the three-dimensional world like humans. This is crucial for applications ranging from self-driving cars navigating complex urban landscapes to robots assembling delicate objects in factories. Advances in stereo vision, where two cameras capture images from slightly different angles, and structure from motion, where a sequence of images reveals depth information, are paving the way for machines to perceive depth with increasing accuracy.

Beyond depth perception, the future of computer vision lies in scene understanding, where machines can go beyond simply recognizing objects to comprehending the context and relationships within a scene. Imagine a machine that can interpret a bustling city street, understanding the flow of traffic, the actions of pedestrians, and the significance of various objects in the environment. Such capabilities will open up new possibilities for applications like smart city management, autonomous navigation, and even creative artistic endeavors.

To achieve scene understanding, computer vision research is pushing the boundaries of object detection and tracking, enabling machines to identify and follow the movement of objects in real-time. This involves training algorithms to recognize patterns and relationships between objects, their movements, and the overall scene context.

Another critical aspect of scene understanding is image segmentation, which involves dividing an image into meaningful regions. This allows machines to identify different objects, distinguish between foreground and background, and understand the spatial relationships between objects. Imagine a machine that can understand a complex scene like a forest, recognizing different trees, identifying animal trails, and even detecting potential signs of environmental changes.

The future of computer vision is also deeply intertwined with human-computer interaction, enabling more natural and intuitive ways for humans to interact with machines. This involves developing systems that can understand human gestures, facial expressions, and even the subtle nuances of our gaze.

One exciting area of research is gaze estimation, where machines can analyze eye movements to understand a person's attention and intent. This technology can enhance human-computer interaction, allowing machines to anticipate user needs, personalize experiences, and even provide assistance in specific tasks. Imagine a computer interface that adapts to your gaze, highlighting relevant information and navigating you through complex tasks based on your visual focus.

Another promising area is gesture recognition, enabling machines to interpret human gestures and translate them into commands or actions. This can lead to more natural and intuitive ways to control devices, such as manipulating virtual objects, navigating through menus, or even controlling robots. Imagine a world where you can control your smartphone with just a wave of your hand or interact with a robot by simply pointing to an object.

Furthermore, the intersection of computer vision and artificial intelligence (AI) is unlocking new possibilities for human-computer collaboration. AI algorithms can be used to interpret complex visual information, generate creative content, and even assist in decision-making processes. Imagine a world where AI-powered assistants can analyze medical images, provide expert advice in financial markets, or even create captivating artwork based on your input.

The future of computer vision is not just about technological advancements; it's about enhancing our understanding of the world, enabling us to perceive and interact with it in more meaningful ways. As computer vision continues to evolve, it promises to transform how we live, work, and connect with each other, opening up a world of new possibilities that are just beginning to take shape.

Examples of Computer Vision Applications Shaping the Future

Here are some specific examples of how computer vision is already transforming various industries and our everyday lives:

Healthcare

- **Automated Diagnosis:** Computer vision algorithms are being trained to analyze medical images, such as X-rays, MRIs, and CT scans, to identify tumors, diagnose diseases, and assist doctors in making more accurate diagnoses.
- **Personalized Treatment:** AI-powered systems can analyze patient data, including medical images, to personalize treatment plans and optimize medication dosages.
- **Surgical Assistance:** Robotic surgical systems equipped with advanced computer vision capabilities can assist surgeons in performing delicate procedures with greater precision and accuracy.

Transportation

- **Self-Driving Cars:** Computer vision is at the heart of self-driving cars, enabling them to perceive their surroundings, identify objects and pedestrians, and navigate roads safely and efficiently.
- **Traffic Management:** AI algorithms are being used to analyze traffic patterns, optimize traffic flow, and reduce congestion in cities.
- **Automated Parking:** Computer vision systems can assist drivers in finding parking spaces, guiding them

to available spots, and even enabling automated parking.

Retail

- **Enhanced Shopping Experience:** Computer vision can personalize the shopping experience by identifying customer preferences, suggesting relevant products, and providing interactive product information.
- **Inventory Management:** AI-powered systems can analyze store cameras to track inventory levels, detect stockouts, and optimize inventory management.
- **Loss Prevention:** Computer vision systems can identify suspicious behavior and potential shoplifting attempts, enhancing security and loss prevention.

Security and Law Enforcement

- **Facial Recognition:** Computer vision systems can identify individuals based on their facial features, improving security measures and aiding in law enforcement investigations.
- **Object Detection:** AI algorithms can detect suspicious objects in security footage, such as weapons or explosives, enhancing security and preventing potential threats.
- **Crime Scene Investigation:** Computer vision can be used to analyze crime scene photos and videos, identify potential clues, and assist investigators in solving crimes.

Beyond These Industries

- **Robotics:** Computer vision enables robots to interact with their surroundings, navigate complex environments, and perform tasks with greater precision and dexterity.
- **Agriculture:** AI systems can analyze aerial imagery to assess crop health, identify pests and diseases, and optimize farming practices.
- **Environmental Monitoring:** Computer vision can be used to monitor wildlife populations, detect environmental changes, and analyze satellite imagery to track deforestation and climate change.
- **Art and Creativity:** Computer vision is being used to create new forms of art, analyze existing artworks, and inspire creative expression.

Challenges and Ethical Considerations

While the future of computer vision is filled with exciting possibilities, there are also significant challenges and ethical considerations that need to be addressed:

- **Bias and Fairness:** AI algorithms are trained on vast amounts of data, and if this data reflects existing societal biases, the algorithms may perpetuate and even amplify these biases. It is crucial to develop techniques to mitigate bias and ensure fairness in computer vision applications.
- **Privacy and Security:** Computer vision systems often involve the collection and analysis of personal data, raising concerns about privacy and security. We need to develop robust safeguards to protect individual privacy and prevent misuse of this data.

- **Job Displacement:** As computer vision automates tasks previously performed by humans, it raises concerns about job displacement. We need to think about how to mitigate these impacts and ensure a smooth transition for workers.
- **Weaponization:** The potential for weaponizing computer vision technologies raises serious ethical concerns. It is essential to develop guidelines and regulations to prevent the misuse of these technologies for harmful purposes.

Building a Future Where AI Serves Humanity

As computer vision continues to advance, it is essential to prioritize its ethical and responsible development. This involves ensuring that AI systems are fair, unbiased, and accountable. It also requires open dialogue and collaboration between technologists, policymakers, and society as a whole to shape a future where AI serves humanity and creates a better world for everyone.

The future of computer vision is a journey of discovery, innovation, and collaboration. By addressing the challenges and embracing ethical development, we can unlock the full potential of computer vision to create a world where machines see, understand, and interact with the world in ways that benefit all of humanity.

Chapter 6

AI in Finance

Automating Investment

The world of finance is undergoing a dramatic transformation, fueled by the unprecedented capabilities of artificial intelligence (AI). From automating investment decisions to detecting fraudulent activities, AI is revolutionizing every facet of the financial industry. This chapter delves into the fascinating world of AI in finance, exploring how it's reshaping the financial landscape and paving the way for a more efficient, secure, and personalized financial experience.

6.1 AI in Algorithmic Trading: Automating Investment Decisions

The financial markets, driven by constant fluctuations and intricate patterns, have always been a complex and challenging environment for investors. Traditional methods of investment rely heavily on human intuition, experience, and market analysis. However, the rise of AI has introduced a new paradigm in trading – algorithmic trading, where computers execute trades based on pre-defined rules and algorithms.

Algorithmic trading, powered by AI, leverages sophisticated algorithms that analyze vast amounts of data at lightning speed, identifying patterns and opportunities that may be missed by human traders. These algorithms can be programmed to react to specific market conditions, execute trades at optimal times, and manage risk in a more systematic and efficient manner.

The Power of AI in Algorithmic Trading

- **Speed and Efficiency:** AI algorithms can process and analyze market data at speeds far exceeding human capabilities, enabling them to identify fleeting opportunities and execute trades with remarkable precision.
- **Data-Driven Insights:** AI systems can sift through massive datasets, extracting meaningful patterns and insights that may be obscured to the human eye. This allows for more informed and data-driven trading decisions.
- **Risk Management:** AI algorithms can be programmed to incorporate risk management rules, helping traders mitigate potential losses and optimize portfolio performance.
- **Automated Execution:** AI systems can execute trades automatically, eliminating the need for human intervention and ensuring that trades are executed at the most favorable moments.

Types of AI Algorithms in Algorithmic Trading

- **Machine Learning Algorithms:** Machine learning algorithms, trained on historical market data, can learn to predict future price movements and identify profitable trading opportunities. This includes techniques like:
- **Regression Models:** Used to predict continuous values, such as stock prices or asset returns.
- **Classification Models:** Used to categorize assets or market conditions, such as identifying bullish or bearish trends.
- **Deep Learning Algorithms:** Deep learning, a subfield of machine learning, leverages artificial neural networks to process complex data and learn intricate patterns. This allows for more sophisticated and accurate predictions in algorithmic trading.
- **Reinforcement Learning Algorithms:** Reinforcement learning algorithms learn through trial and error, adjusting their trading strategies based on feedback from the market. This enables AI systems to adapt to changing market conditions and develop more effective trading approaches.

Benefits of AI in Algorithmic Trading

- **Increased Efficiency:** AI-powered algorithms can automate trading processes, freeing up traders to focus on higher-level tasks like portfolio management and strategic planning.
- **Enhanced Accuracy:** AI algorithms can analyze data more comprehensively and identify subtle patterns that may be missed by human traders, leading to more accurate predictions and trading decisions.

- **Reduced Emotions and Biases:** Human traders are susceptible to emotional biases and market sentiment, which can lead to irrational trading decisions. AI algorithms, being devoid of emotions, can execute trades based purely on objective data and pre-defined rules.
- **24/7 Trading:** AI systems can operate continuously, monitoring markets around the clock and executing trades even when human traders are not available.

Challenges and Considerations in AI Algorithmic Trading

While AI presents a wealth of opportunities in algorithmic trading, it's essential to acknowledge the challenges and considerations associated with this technology:

- **Data Quality and Availability:** The performance of AI algorithms depends heavily on the quality and availability of training data. Inaccurate or incomplete data can lead to biased algorithms and suboptimal trading decisions.
- **Market Volatility and Uncertainty:** Financial markets are inherently volatile and unpredictable. AI algorithms, while powerful, cannot perfectly predict market movements or eliminate all risks.
- **Black Box Problem:** Some AI algorithms, particularly deep learning models, are considered "black boxes" because their decision-making processes are not easily interpretable. This can make it challenging to understand the rationale behind their actions and identify potential biases.

- **Regulation and Ethics:** The use of AI in algorithmic trading raises ethical and regulatory concerns. Questions arise regarding transparency, accountability, and the potential for market manipulation.

Real-World Examples of AI in Algorithmic Trading

- **Quantitative Hedge Funds:** Many hedge funds employ AI algorithms to manage their investments, analyze market data, and identify trading opportunities. These funds are known for their data-driven approach and sophisticated AI strategies.
- **High-Frequency Trading:** High-frequency trading firms utilize AI algorithms to execute trades at lightning speed, taking advantage of minute price fluctuations and market inefficiencies.
- **Personalized Trading Platforms:** Some online trading platforms offer AI-powered features that provide personalized investment recommendations, risk assessments, and portfolio management tools.

The Future of AI in Algorithmic Trading

The use of AI in algorithmic trading is rapidly evolving, with new techniques and algorithms being developed constantly. Future trends include:

- **Reinforcement Learning:** Reinforcement learning is becoming increasingly popular in algorithmic trading, allowing AI systems to adapt and learn from real-time market data.

- **Explainable AI (XAI):** Research in explainable AI aims to make AI algorithms more transparent and interpretable, addressing the "black box" problem and fostering trust in their decision-making.
- **Hybrid AI Models:** Combining AI algorithms with human expertise can create more robust and efficient trading strategies, leveraging the strengths of both human intuition and AI's data processing capabilities.

As AI continues to advance, its impact on algorithmic trading will only grow, shaping the future of the financial markets and redefining the way we invest and trade. From automating decision-making to enhancing risk management and personalized investing, AI is transforming the financial landscape, paving the way for a more efficient, data-driven, and secure financial future.

Safeguarding Financial Transactions

Fraud is a pervasive problem in the financial world, costing institutions and individuals billions of dollars annually. Traditional fraud detection methods often struggle to keep up with the evolving tactics of criminals. This is where AI steps in, offering a powerful and adaptive solution to combat financial fraud. AI-powered fraud detection systems leverage the power of machine learning algorithms to analyze vast amounts of financial data, identify suspicious patterns, and flag potentially fraudulent transactions in real-time.

Imagine a complex web of financial transactions flowing through a bank's systems every second. It's like a bustling city, with transactions moving in and out, connecting different accounts, and representing a multitude of activities. Humans, even with the best intentions, can't possibly keep track of every transaction, every connection, and every subtle deviation from the norm. That's where AI comes in, acting as an eagle-eyed observer, meticulously analyzing the intricate network of financial data for any signs of fraud.

Machine learning algorithms, the core of these AI systems, are trained on massive datasets of historical financial transactions, both legitimate and fraudulent. By analyzing these data, the algorithms learn to distinguish between typical and suspicious patterns. They look for anomalies, inconsistencies, and unusual relationships that could indicate fraudulent activity. For example, a sudden increase in the frequency of transactions from a particular account, a transaction originating from a high-risk region, or an unusually large transfer to a previously inactive account might trigger an alert.

The power of AI in fraud detection lies in its ability to adapt and learn. Unlike rule-based systems, which rely on predefined criteria, machine learning algorithms constantly evolve based on the data they encounter. They can identify new fraud patterns and adapt to evolving criminal tactics, ensuring their effectiveness in a dynamic financial landscape.

Let's delve into some specific examples to illustrate the capabilities of AI in fraud detection:

- **Credit Card Fraud:** AI can identify fraudulent credit card transactions by analyzing spending patterns, transaction locations, and the time of day. If a credit card is suddenly used in a location far from its usual usage area, or if there's a surge in purchases significantly exceeding the cardholder's typical spending habits, the AI system can raise an alarm.

- **Online Payment Fraud:** AI can detect fraudulent online payments by analyzing user behavior, device information, and transaction history. If a transaction originates from a new device or IP address, or if there's a mismatch between the billing address and the shipping address, the system might flag it as suspicious.
- **Money Laundering:** AI can assist in identifying money laundering activities by analyzing complex networks of financial transactions. By identifying suspicious patterns in cross-border payments, unusual account activity, and transactions involving multiple accounts, AI systems can help investigators uncover and dismantle money laundering schemes.
- **Identity Theft:** AI can help detect identity theft by analyzing personal data, such as social security numbers, addresses, and credit card information. If there's a sudden change in an individual's address, multiple credit applications, or unusual credit card activity, the AI system can trigger an alert.

AI-powered fraud detection systems are designed to be highly scalable, capable of handling the immense volume of data generated by modern financial institutions. They can process transactions in real-time, providing instant alerts to investigators, enabling swift action to prevent financial losses. These systems can also automate investigations, significantly reducing the workload of human analysts and allowing them to focus on more complex cases.

However, the use of AI in fraud detection isn't without its challenges. One major concern is the potential for bias in AI algorithms. If training data is biased, the algorithms might inadvertently discriminate against certain groups, leading to false positives and unfair outcomes. It's crucial to ensure that training datasets are diverse, representative, and free from biases to mitigate this risk.

Another challenge is the interpretability of AI models. AI systems often operate as "black boxes," making it difficult to understand why they arrive at certain conclusions. This lack of transparency can hinder trust and accountability in the decision-making process. Researchers are actively working on developing more transparent AI algorithms and tools to provide insights into the reasoning behind their predictions.

Despite these challenges, the potential of AI in fraud detection is undeniable. As technology continues to evolve, AI-powered systems are expected to become even more sophisticated, adaptive, and effective in combating financial fraud. They will continue to play a critical role in safeguarding financial transactions, protecting individuals and institutions from the devastating consequences of fraud.

Furthermore, the integration of AI into financial systems presents opportunities for collaboration and innovation. Financial institutions can work together to share data, enhance training datasets, and develop collaborative fraud detection systems. This shared intelligence can amplify the effectiveness of fraud prevention, creating a more secure financial landscape.

Looking ahead, the future of AI in fraud detection holds exciting possibilities. AI systems are expected to incorporate advanced technologies like natural language processing, computer vision, and blockchain to enhance their capabilities. They can analyze unstructured data, such as social media posts and website content, to identify potential threats and predict fraudulent activities. The combination of AI and blockchain technology can also create a more secure and transparent financial ecosystem, reducing the risks of fraud and enhancing trust in online transactions.

The battle against financial fraud is ongoing, and AI is emerging as a formidable weapon in this fight. As AI continues to evolve and become more integrated into financial systems, it has the potential to transform the way we detect and prevent fraud, creating a more secure and resilient financial world for all.

Tailoring Solutions to Individuals Needs

Imagine a world where your financial advisor understands your dreams, your fears, and your unique financial situation better than you do. This is the promise of AI in personalized financial services, a realm where algorithms analyze vast amounts of data to tailor financial solutions precisely to your individual needs.

The power of AI lies in its ability to learn and adapt. It can analyze your spending patterns, income, and investment goals, identifying trends and opportunities that you might miss. It can also sift through mountains of financial data, from market trends to economic indicators, to generate insights and predictions that inform investment strategies.

AI in Investment Advice

Traditionally, financial advice has often been a one-size-fits-all approach, relying on generic strategies and broad market recommendations. AI, however, empowers a more personalized approach. AI-powered investment platforms can analyze your risk tolerance, investment goals, and time horizon to create customized investment portfolios that align with your individual needs.

For example, an AI-driven robo-advisor can assess your financial situation and create a diversified portfolio of stocks, bonds, and other assets that match your risk profile. It can also automatically adjust your portfolio as market conditions change, ensuring your investments remain aligned with your goals.

AI in Loan Applications

Applying for a loan can be a stressful and time-consuming process. AI is changing this landscape by streamlining loan applications and providing faster, more accurate decisions. AI algorithms can analyze vast amounts of data, including your credit history, income, and employment information, to assess your creditworthiness and make loan decisions in real time.

For example, AI-powered loan applications can evaluate your creditworthiness based on alternative data, such as your social media activity or online shopping patterns, offering access to credit for individuals who might otherwise be overlooked by traditional lending institutions. This can be particularly beneficial for individuals with limited credit histories, such as young adults or new immigrants.

AI in Insurance Policies

The insurance industry is also embracing AI to offer more personalized and affordable policies. AI algorithms can analyze your driving history, medical records, and other relevant data to assess your risk profile and tailor insurance premiums accordingly.

For instance, AI-powered insurance platforms can offer discounts based on safe driving behavior, such as using telematics devices to track your driving habits. AI can also identify potential health risks based on your medical records and lifestyle factors, enabling insurers to offer more personalized and affordable health insurance plans.

Beyond the Basics: AI's Expanding Role in Personalized Finance

Beyond investment advice, loan applications, and insurance policies, AI is making its mark in a wide range of financial services. AI-powered chatbots are transforming customer service, providing instant answers to common financial questions and resolving issues more efficiently. AI is also playing a critical role in fraud detection, identifying suspicious transactions and protecting financial institutions and customers from fraud.

The Benefits of AI in Personalized Finance

The benefits of AI in personalized finance are numerous:

- **Increased Efficiency:** AI streamlines processes, from loan applications to investment portfolio management, saving time and reducing costs.
- **Improved Accuracy:** AI algorithms can analyze vast amounts of data to provide more accurate financial insights and predictions.
- **Personalized Solutions:** AI tailors financial solutions to meet the unique needs of each individual, providing more relevant and effective advice.
- **Enhanced Accessibility:** AI makes financial services more accessible to individuals with limited resources or credit histories, promoting financial inclusion.

- **Greater Transparency:** AI can provide greater transparency into financial decisions, empowering individuals to understand and control their finances.

The Ethical Considerations of AI in Finance

While AI offers significant benefits, it is essential to address ethical concerns. These include:

- **Bias and Discrimination:** AI algorithms can perpetuate existing biases if they are trained on data that reflects discriminatory practices. It is crucial to develop AI systems that are fair, impartial, and unbiased.
- **Privacy and Security:** AI relies on vast amounts of personal data, raising concerns about privacy and security. Robust safeguards are necessary to protect sensitive financial information from unauthorized access and misuse.
- **Job Displacement:** AI's increasing automation capabilities raise concerns about job displacement in the financial sector. It is essential to plan for the transition to a workforce that incorporates AI technologies while ensuring retraining and support for displaced workers.

The Future of AI in Personalized Finance

The future of AI in personalized finance is bright. As AI technology continues to evolve, we can expect even more sophisticated and personalized financial services. AI will likely play a critical role in:

- **Financial Planning:** AI will assist in creating comprehensive financial plans, considering factors such as retirement planning, education savings, and estate planning.
- **Wealth Management:** AI will offer sophisticated wealth management solutions, including portfolio optimization, risk management, and tax planning.
- **Financial Education:** AI will provide accessible and personalized financial education, empowering individuals to make informed financial decisions.
- **Financial Inclusion:** AI will help bridge the gap in access to financial services, providing opportunities for individuals who have historically been excluded.

A New Era of Financial Empowerment

AI is ushering in a new era of financial empowerment, where individuals have access to personalized financial solutions that meet their unique needs. While ethical considerations remain paramount, AI's potential to transform the financial landscape is undeniable. By embracing AI responsibly and thoughtfully, we can create a more inclusive and equitable financial future for all.

Assessing and Mitigating Financial Risks

AI in Risk Management: Assessing and Mitigating Financial Risks

The financial world is inherently intertwined with risk. From stock market fluctuations to credit defaults, financial institutions constantly grapple with the unpredictable nature of markets and the potential for losses. Traditional risk management practices often rely on historical data and human expertise, but these methods can be slow, prone to bias, and limited in their ability to anticipate emerging threats. This is where AI steps in, offering a transformative approach to risk management that leverages the power of data analysis, predictive modeling, and automation.

AI-powered risk management tools are changing the way financial institutions assess, monitor, and mitigate financial risks. These tools use sophisticated algorithms and machine learning techniques to analyze vast amounts of data, identify potential risks, and develop strategies for minimizing their impact. The key to AI's success in risk management lies in its ability to:

- **Identify patterns and anomalies:** AI algorithms can analyze historical data, market trends, and real-time information to detect subtle patterns and anomalies that might escape human observation. For example, AI can flag unusual trading activity, identify early warning signs of credit defaults, or detect potential fraud attempts.
- **Predict future events:** By leveraging machine learning, AI can build predictive models that forecast potential risks based on historical data and current market conditions. These models can help institutions anticipate market volatility, estimate the likelihood of loan defaults, or predict the impact of regulatory changes.
- **Optimize risk mitigation strategies:** AI algorithms can analyze different risk mitigation strategies and develop tailored solutions that minimize risk exposure while maximizing returns. For instance, AI can recommend optimal portfolio allocations, identify

opportunities for hedging, or suggest adjustments to credit scoring models.

AI in Action: Real-World Examples

The application of AI in risk management is becoming increasingly common across various financial sectors:

- **Credit risk management:** Banks and financial institutions are using AI to assess creditworthiness and predict loan defaults. AI algorithms analyze data from credit history, financial statements, and online behavior to build more accurate risk profiles and identify potential borrowers who are at higher risk.
- **Market risk management:** Hedge funds and investment banks are employing AI to analyze market data, identify trading opportunities, and manage portfolio risk. AI-powered trading algorithms can execute trades at lightning speed, capitalizing on fleeting market opportunities and minimizing exposure to volatility.
- **Operational risk management:** AI is being used to detect and prevent operational errors, such as fraud, data breaches, and system failures. AI algorithms can monitor transactions, identify suspicious activity, and flag potential vulnerabilities in internal processes.
- **Regulatory risk management:** Financial institutions are leveraging AI to comply with complex regulations and anticipate changes in regulatory frameworks. AI algorithms can analyze legal documents, interpret regulations, and assess the impact of potential regulatory changes on their operations.

Benefits of AI in Risk Management

The integration of AI into risk management processes offers several significant benefits:

- **Enhanced accuracy and efficiency:** AI algorithms can analyze data much faster and more accurately than humans, leading to more reliable risk assessments and more efficient risk mitigation strategies.
- **Proactive risk management:** AI can identify potential risks early on, allowing institutions to take timely actions to minimize their impact.
- **Improved decision-making:** AI provides financial professionals with data-driven insights and recommendations, improving their decision-making capabilities and enhancing risk management strategies.
- **Reduced operational costs:** By automating routine tasks and processes, AI can help financial institutions streamline their risk management operations and reduce operational costs.
- **Increased transparency and accountability:** AI-powered risk management systems can provide clear and detailed documentation of risk assessments, mitigation strategies, and decision-making processes, enhancing transparency and accountability.

Challenges and Ethical Considerations

Despite its potential benefits, the adoption of AI in risk management also poses certain challenges and raises ethical considerations:

- **Data quality and availability:** The accuracy and effectiveness of AI models rely heavily on the quality and availability of data. Financial institutions need to ensure that their data is reliable, comprehensive, and representative.
- **Algorithmic bias:** AI algorithms can inherit biases from the data they are trained on. This can lead to discriminatory outcomes and unfair risk assessments. Financial institutions need to carefully evaluate their AI models for biases and implement measures to mitigate them.
- **Interpretability and explainability:** While AI models can make accurate predictions, it can be challenging to understand how they arrived at those predictions. This lack of transparency can make it difficult to trust and explain AI-driven decisions.
- **Job displacement:** The automation of risk management tasks through AI could lead to job displacement in the financial industry. Financial institutions need to consider the social impact of AI and invest in retraining and upskilling their workforce.
- **Ethical considerations:** As AI plays a more significant role in risk management, it is crucial to address ethical considerations, such as data privacy, responsible use of algorithms, and the potential for unintended consequences.

The Future of AI in Risk Management

The future of AI in risk management holds great promise. As AI technology continues to evolve, we can expect to see even more sophisticated and powerful risk management tools. These tools will be able to:

- **Analyze data from multiple sources:** AI models will be able to integrate data from various sources, including internal systems, external databases, social media, and news feeds, providing a more holistic view of risks.
- **Develop more complex and accurate predictive models:** Advanced machine learning techniques, such as deep learning and reinforcement learning, will enable the development of more powerful predictive models that can anticipate risks with greater accuracy.
- **Personalize risk management strategies:** AI will be able to tailor risk management strategies to individual clients and their specific financial needs and risk tolerance.
- **Enhance cybersecurity and fraud detection:** AI will play a crucial role in protecting financial institutions from cyber threats and fraud, by continuously monitoring systems, detecting anomalies, and identifying malicious activity.

CONCLUSION

AI is transforming the financial landscape, and risk management is no exception. AI-powered tools are offering financial institutions a powerful arsenal of capabilities to assess, monitor, and mitigate financial risks. By leveraging the power of data analysis, predictive modeling, and automation, AI can help institutions identify risks earlier, make more informed decisions, and optimize their risk mitigation strategies. However, it is essential to address the challenges and ethical considerations associated with AI, ensuring that its implementation is responsible, transparent, and beneficial for all stakeholders. As AI technology continues to evolve, its role in risk management is likely to become even more prominent, shaping the future of finance and driving innovation in the years to come.

Shaping the Future

The financial landscape is undergoing a profound transformation, driven by the rise of artificial intelligence (AI). From automating investment decisions to safeguarding transactions and personalizing financial services, AI is revolutionizing every aspect of the industry. This chapter delves into the potential impact of AI on the future of finance, exploring how advancements in blockchain technology, decentralized finance, and digital currencies are shaping the future of money itself.

6.5.1. Blockchain Technology: Disrupting the Financial Infrastructure

Blockchain technology, the foundation of cryptocurrencies like Bitcoin, is a revolutionary innovation that has the potential to disrupt the traditional financial infrastructure. At its core, a blockchain is a distributed ledger that records transactions across a network of computers, ensuring transparency, security, and immutability. These features make blockchain technology a game-changer in finance, promising a more efficient, secure, and inclusive financial system.

- **Enhanced Transparency:** Blockchain's distributed ledger eliminates the need for central authorities, allowing for greater transparency in transactions. Each transaction is recorded and accessible to all participants in the network, fostering trust and accountability. This transparency can help combat financial fraud, improve regulatory oversight, and increase investor confidence.

- **Unparalleled Security:** Blockchain technology is inherently secure due to its decentralized nature and cryptography. Transactions are encrypted and verified by multiple nodes in the network, making them highly resistant to tampering and hacking. This security is particularly relevant in finance, where safeguarding sensitive data and preventing fraudulent activities is paramount.
- **Streamlined Efficiency:** Blockchain technology streamlines financial processes, reducing the time and cost associated with traditional intermediaries like banks. By automating tasks like settlements and clearing, blockchain can accelerate transactions and reduce friction in the financial system.
- **Increased Accessibility:** Blockchain technology can extend financial services to underserved populations, particularly in emerging markets. By creating a decentralized and open financial system, blockchain can empower individuals without access to traditional banking services to participate in the global economy.

Examples

- **Cross-border Payments:** Blockchain can facilitate faster and cheaper cross-border payments, eliminating the need for intermediaries and reducing transaction fees.

- **Trade Finance:** Blockchain can streamline trade finance processes, improving transparency, security, and efficiency in global trade.
- **Supply Chain Management:** Blockchain can track goods and materials throughout the supply chain, improving transparency and accountability.
- **Digital Identity:** Blockchain can create secure and tamper-proof digital identities, enabling individuals to control their personal data and privacy.

6.5.2. Decentralized Finance (DeFi): Empowering Financial Inclusion

Decentralized finance (DeFi) is a rapidly growing movement leveraging blockchain technology to create a more inclusive and accessible financial system. DeFi applications aim to replace traditional financial intermediaries with automated protocols and smart contracts, allowing for direct peer-to-peer transactions and financial services.

- **Open Access:** DeFi applications are open to anyone with an internet connection, regardless of their location or credit history. This accessibility empowers individuals and communities previously excluded from traditional financial systems.
- **Transparent and Secure:** DeFi protocols are built on open-source code and run on decentralized networks, ensuring transparency and security. Transactions are recorded on blockchains, providing an auditable trail for all participants.
- **Financial Innovation:** DeFi encourages innovation by allowing developers to build new financial products

and services without relying on intermediaries. This fosters competition and drives rapid advancements in the financial landscape.

Examples

- **Lending and Borrowing:** DeFi platforms allow individuals to lend and borrow cryptocurrencies directly from each other, without the need for banks or other intermediaries.
- **Stablecoins:** DeFi stablecoins are cryptocurrencies pegged to fiat currencies like the US dollar, providing a more stable asset class for DeFi applications.
- **Decentralized Exchanges:** DeFi decentralized exchanges (DEXs) allow individuals to trade cryptocurrencies directly with each other, without reliance on centralized exchanges.
- **Yield Farming:** DeFi protocols allow users to earn interest on their cryptocurrencies by lending them out or participating in liquidity pools.

6.5.3. Digital Currencies: The Future of Money

Digital currencies, particularly cryptocurrencies like Bitcoin and Ethereum, are rapidly gaining popularity and are poised to transform the way we think about money. These digital assets offer unique features that challenge the traditional financial system and open up new possibilities for financial transactions.

- **Decentralization:** Digital currencies are not controlled by any central authority, making them resistant to government intervention and censorship.

- **Programmability:** Digital currencies can be programmed to execute specific functions, enabling the creation of smart contracts and decentralized applications (dApps).
- **Global Accessibility:** Digital currencies can be transferred across borders easily and quickly, making them a convenient option for international transactions.
- **Emerging Use Cases:** Beyond payments, digital currencies are finding new applications in areas such as identity verification, supply chain management, and digital asset ownership.

Examples

- **Bitcoin:** The first and most well-known cryptocurrency, Bitcoin is a decentralized digital currency with a limited supply.
- **Ethereum:** Ethereum is a blockchain platform that enables the creation and deployment of smart contracts and dApps.
- **Stablecoins:** Stablecoins like Tether (USDT) and USD Coin (USDC) are cryptocurrencies pegged to fiat currencies, providing stability and price predictability.
- **Central Bank Digital Currencies (CBDCs):** Governments around the world are exploring the development of central bank digital currencies (CBDCs), which would offer the benefits of digital currencies while being backed by the government.

6.5.4. The Intersection of AI, Blockchain, and Decentralized Finance

The convergence of AI, blockchain, and decentralized finance is creating a powerful synergy that is reshaping the financial landscape. AI-powered algorithms are being integrated into DeFi protocols, enabling more efficient and intelligent financial services.

- **AI-Driven Risk Assessment:** AI algorithms can analyze vast datasets to assess risk more effectively than traditional methods. This enables DeFi protocols to offer more accurate and personalized lending and borrowing terms.
- **Automated Trading:** AI algorithms can automate trading strategies in DeFi markets, optimizing portfolio management and maximizing returns.
- **Fraud Detection and Prevention:** AI can identify fraudulent activities on decentralized networks, safeguarding user funds and maintaining the integrity of DeFi protocols.
- **Personalized Financial Services:** AI can personalize financial services based on individual preferences and risk profiles, providing more tailored solutions for users.

Examples

- **AI-powered lending platforms:** DeFi platforms are incorporating AI algorithms to assess borrower creditworthiness and provide more accurate lending terms.
- **Automated portfolio management:** AI-powered tools can optimize investment portfolios based on individual goals and risk tolerances.

- **Smart contract auditing:** AI algorithms can analyze smart contracts for vulnerabilities and security flaws, ensuring the integrity of DeFi protocols.

6.5.5. Regulatory Landscape and Ethical Considerations

The rapid advancements in AI, blockchain, and DeFi have raised significant regulatory and ethical considerations. As these technologies continue to evolve, it is crucial to develop robust regulatory frameworks that balance innovation with consumer protection and financial stability.

- **Data Privacy and Security:** The use of AI in finance raises concerns about data privacy and security. Regulatory frameworks need to ensure that sensitive financial data is collected, used, and stored responsibly.
- **Algorithmic Bias:** AI algorithms can perpetuate biases present in the data they are trained on. It is essential to address algorithmic bias to prevent discrimination and ensure fair and equitable access to financial services.
- **Financial Stability:** The emergence of DeFi and digital currencies has introduced new challenges to financial stability. Regulators need to develop mechanisms to monitor and manage systemic risks associated with these technologies.
- **Consumer Protection:** Regulatory frameworks should protect consumers from fraud, manipulation, and other risks associated with AI-powered financial services.

Examples

- **The European Union's General Data Protection Regulation (GDPR):** The GDPR sets out comprehensive rules for data privacy and protection, including specific provisions for AI applications.
- **The Financial Stability Board's (FSB) recommendations on crypto-assets:** The FSB has issued recommendations on the regulation of crypto-assets to address potential risks to financial stability.
- **The U.S. Securities and Exchange Commission (SEC) regulations on digital asset offerings:** The SEC has issued regulations to govern the offering and trading of digital assets.

6.5.6. The Future of Money: Embracing a Decentralized and Intelligent Future

The future of finance is likely to be shaped by the convergence of AI, blockchain, and decentralized finance. These technologies have the potential to revolutionize the way we interact with money, creating a more efficient, secure, and inclusive financial system.

- **Increased Financial Inclusion:** Blockchain and DeFi technologies have the potential to empower individuals and communities previously excluded from traditional financial systems, fostering greater financial inclusion and economic opportunity.
- **Enhanced Security and Transparency:** AI-powered fraud detection systems and blockchain's immutable ledger can significantly enhance the security and transparency of financial transactions, reducing fraud and increasing trust in the system.

- **Personalized Financial Services:** AI algorithms can personalize financial services based on individual preferences and risk profiles, providing more tailored solutions and improving customer satisfaction.
- **Emerging Opportunities for Innovation:** The combination of AI, blockchain, and DeFi is opening up new opportunities for financial innovation, enabling the creation of novel financial products and services that address current and future needs.

The future of finance is not without its challenges, but the potential benefits of AI, blockchain, and DeFi are too significant to ignore. By embracing these technologies responsibly, we can create a more efficient, secure, and inclusive financial system that benefits all of society.

Chapter 7

AI in Healthcare

Revolutionizing Medical Practices

Assisting Medical Professionals

Imagine a world where doctors can diagnose diseases with unparalleled accuracy, predict potential complications before they arise, and tailor treatment plans specifically to each patient's unique needs. This isn't science fiction; it's the reality that Artificial Intelligence (AI) is rapidly bringing to healthcare. AI is transforming medical practices, empowering doctors with powerful tools to make better decisions, improve patient outcomes, and ultimately, create a healthier future for all.

The application of AI in diagnosis and treatment is at the forefront of this revolution. Doctors are increasingly relying on AI-powered systems to assist them in making informed and timely decisions. These systems analyze vast amounts of medical data, including patient histories, medical images, and research publications, to identify patterns and insights that human eyes may miss. This allows doctors to quickly pinpoint the root cause of a patient's ailment, identify potential complications, and recommend the most effective treatment options.

One of the most significant advancements in AI-assisted diagnosis is the use of deep learning algorithms to analyze medical images. These algorithms can detect subtle abnormalities in X-rays, MRIs, and other scans that might escape the attention of even the most experienced radiologist. This is particularly crucial in identifying early stages of diseases, when timely intervention can drastically improve treatment outcomes. For example, AI-powered systems are being used to detect breast cancer in mammograms with greater accuracy than human radiologists. They can also analyze retinal scans to detect early signs of diabetic retinopathy, a leading cause of blindness.

Beyond image analysis, AI is being employed to predict potential complications and personalize treatment plans. By analyzing a patient's medical history, genetic information, and other relevant data, AI algorithms can identify patients at risk of developing specific conditions. This allows doctors to intervene early, taking preventative measures to mitigate the risk of complications. Moreover, AI can recommend personalized treatment plans that consider a patient's unique biology, lifestyle, and preferences, enhancing the effectiveness and adherence to treatment.

For instance, in the field of oncology, AI is being used to predict the response of cancer cells to specific chemotherapy drugs. This enables doctors to select the most effective treatment for each patient, minimizing the risk of side effects and maximizing the chances of remission. Similarly, AI is being used in cardiovascular disease management to predict the risk of heart attacks and strokes, allowing for early interventions to prevent these life-threatening events.

The application of AI in diagnosis and treatment isn't limited to specific disease areas. It's revolutionizing various aspects of healthcare delivery, making it more efficient, accurate, and patient-centered. For example, AI-powered chatbots are being used to provide basic medical advice and support to patients, freeing up doctors to focus on more complex cases. AI systems are also assisting doctors in scheduling appointments, managing patient records, and coordinating care, streamlining the entire healthcare process.

The potential of AI in transforming diagnosis and treatment is vast, but it's essential to acknowledge the ethical considerations that accompany these advancements. It's crucial to ensure that AI systems are developed and used responsibly, avoiding biases that could perpetuate health disparities. Transparent and explainable AI is vital to ensure that doctors understand the reasoning behind the system's recommendations and maintain control over patient care.

Moreover, the integration of AI in healthcare requires a collaborative effort between doctors, AI developers, and healthcare administrators. Open communication and a shared understanding of the capabilities and limitations of AI are essential for its successful implementation. Ultimately, the goal is to leverage AI to empower doctors, not to replace them.

As AI technology continues to advance, its role in healthcare is expected to expand even further. From personalized genomics to drug discovery and robotic surgery, AI has the potential to revolutionize every aspect of medicine. By embracing AI responsibly and collaborating to harness its power, we can create a healthcare system that is more efficient, accurate, and equitable for all.

This is not just about technological advancements; it's about improving the lives of millions of people around the world. By harnessing the power of AI, we can create a future where everyone has access to the best possible healthcare, regardless of their location or socioeconomic status. The revolution is underway, and AI is leading the charge towards a healthier future.

Accelerating the Development of New Medications

Imagine a world where the arduous and time-consuming process of drug discovery is accelerated, where new medications can be developed faster, and where the fight against diseases like cancer and Alzheimer's is bolstered by a revolutionary force. This is the world that AI promises, and at its forefront stands AI-powered drug discovery, a field that leverages the immense capabilities of artificial intelligence to expedite the development of new medications.

Traditional drug discovery is a long and intricate journey, often spanning years and costing billions of dollars. It involves multiple steps, including identifying potential drug targets, designing and synthesizing candidate molecules, testing their efficacy and safety in laboratory settings, and finally conducting clinical trials in humans. Each step is fraught with challenges and uncertainties, making the entire process time-consuming, expensive, and often unsuccessful.

AI enters this complex landscape as a powerful ally, offering a transformative approach to drug discovery that aims to streamline and accelerate the process. By leveraging the power of machine learning, deep learning, and other AI techniques, researchers can now analyze vast amounts of data, identify promising drug targets with greater precision, and design potential drug candidates with enhanced efficacy and safety.

One of the key ways AI is revolutionizing drug discovery is by identifying potential drug targets. These targets are specific molecules, proteins, or pathways within the body that are involved in disease development. Traditional methods for identifying drug targets often rely on painstaking experiments and trial and error, but AI offers a more efficient and data-driven approach.

By analyzing massive datasets of biological information, including genomic data, protein structures, and clinical trial data, AI algorithms can identify patterns and correlations that might otherwise be missed. These algorithms can then predict which molecules are most likely to be effective drug targets, narrowing down the search space and saving time and resources.

For instance, AI algorithms can analyze protein structures to identify pockets that could bind to a drug molecule, effectively predicting which proteins are most likely to be good drug targets. This process, known as target identification, has been significantly enhanced by AI, allowing researchers to prioritize potential targets with greater confidence.

AI also plays a crucial role in designing potential drug candidates, a process known as drug design. Traditional drug design often involves a laborious trial-and-error approach, where chemists synthesize and test numerous molecules to find those with the desired properties. However, AI offers a more intelligent and efficient method.

AI algorithms can use sophisticated models of protein structures and drug-target interactions to predict the effectiveness of potential drug molecules. These algorithms can then generate new drug candidates with desired properties, such as high binding affinity, low toxicity, and good bioavailability. This process, known as virtual screening, has enabled researchers to quickly identify promising drug candidates without needing to synthesize and test them in the lab.

In addition to identifying targets and designing drug candidates, AI is also being used to predict the efficacy of drug candidates. By analyzing data from preclinical and clinical trials, AI algorithms can predict how well a drug will work in humans. This predictive capability is invaluable for optimizing drug development and ensuring that only the most promising candidates proceed to clinical trials.

AI algorithms can analyze data from preclinical studies, such as cell line studies and animal models, to predict a drug's effectiveness in humans. They can also analyze data from clinical trials to identify factors that influence a drug's efficacy, such as patient demographics, genetic makeup, and disease severity. This data-driven approach allows researchers to make more informed decisions about which drug candidates are most likely to succeed in clinical trials.

The impact of AI in drug discovery is already being felt across various sectors. Pharmaceutical companies, biotechnology firms, and academic institutions are actively integrating AI into their drug discovery pipelines. Several AI-powered drug discovery companies have emerged, offering their services to help accelerate the development of new medications.

For example, Exscientia, a leading AI-powered drug discovery company, uses its AI platform to design and identify novel drug candidates. Their AI algorithms have been successful in discovering several potential drugs for a range of diseases, including cancer, inflammatory diseases, and neurodegenerative disorders.

Another notable example is BenevolentAI, a company that utilizes AI to understand complex diseases and identify new drug targets. Their platform uses AI to analyze large datasets of scientific information, identifying potential drug targets that have been overlooked by traditional methods.

The use of AI in drug discovery is not without its challenges. One key concern is the availability of high-quality data. AI algorithms require massive amounts of data to be trained effectively, and the quality of this data is crucial for generating accurate and reliable results.

Another challenge is the interpretability of AI models. While AI algorithms can generate predictions, it can be difficult to understand why they are making those predictions. This lack of transparency can make it challenging to trust the results and build confidence in AI-powered drug discovery.

Despite these challenges, AI is poised to transform the landscape of drug discovery. The potential of AI to accelerate the process, identify promising targets, design effective drug candidates, and predict efficacy is undeniable. As AI continues to evolve and improve, we can expect even greater advancements in drug discovery, ultimately leading to the development of new treatments for diseases that have plagued humanity for centuries.

Here are some additional examples and details to further expand on the topic:

AI-powered target identification:

- Deep learning algorithms can analyze protein structures and identify potential drug targets based on their 3D shape and chemical properties.
- AI algorithms can also analyze genomic data to identify genetic mutations that contribute to disease development, providing valuable insights into potential drug targets.
- Machine learning algorithms can analyze large datasets of patient data to identify correlations between disease progression and specific molecular targets, offering new avenues for drug discovery.

AI-driven drug design:

- Generative adversarial networks (GANs) can be used to generate new drug molecules with desired properties, potentially leading to the discovery of novel and effective drug candidates.
- Reinforcement learning algorithms can be used to optimize the design of drug molecules by learning from previous successes and failures.
- AI algorithms can also be used to predict the physical and chemical properties of drug molecules, helping researchers choose the most promising candidates for further development.

AI-assisted clinical trial design:

- AI algorithms can be used to identify the most relevant patient populations for clinical trials, ensuring that the trials are efficient and successful.

- AI algorithms can also be used to design clinical trial protocols that are more responsive to patient needs and preferences.
- AI can help to automate the collection and analysis of data from clinical trials, enabling researchers to make more informed decisions about drug development.

AI and drug repurposing:

- AI algorithms can be used to identify existing drugs that could be repurposed to treat new diseases, potentially accelerating the development of new therapies.
- AI algorithms can analyze vast databases of drug-disease interactions to identify potential repurposing opportunities, significantly shortening the drug discovery process.
- AI can also be used to predict the potential side effects of repurposed drugs, ensuring the safety of patients.

The transformative power of AI in drug discovery is undeniable. By leveraging the power of machine learning, deep learning, and other AI techniques, researchers can accelerate the process, identify promising targets, design effective drug candidates, and predict efficacy with greater precision. This revolution in drug discovery holds immense promise for the development of new medications and the advancement of healthcare, ultimately contributing to a healthier future for all.

Tailoring Treatment to Individual Patients

Imagine a world where healthcare is no longer a one-size-fits-all approach. Instead, imagine a future where treatments are tailored specifically to each individual, taking into account their unique genetic makeup, lifestyle, and environmental factors. This vision of personalized medicine is becoming a reality thanks to the transformative power of artificial intelligence (AI).

AI is revolutionizing healthcare by analyzing vast amounts of data to identify patterns and insights that would be impossible for humans to discern. This data includes patient records, genomic information, medical literature, and even wearable device readings. AI algorithms can sift through this data to identify risk factors, predict disease progression, and recommend individualized treatment plans.

One of the most promising applications of AI in personalized medicine is the development of precision medicine. Precision medicine aims to tailor treatment to each patient's unique characteristics, ensuring that they receive the most effective and targeted therapies. By analyzing a patient's genetic profile, doctors can identify specific genetic variations that may influence their response to certain drugs or their susceptibility to certain diseases. This information can then be used to design personalized treatment plans that are more likely to be effective and minimize side effects.

For example, AI-powered tools are being used to predict the risk of heart disease based on a patient's genetic profile, lifestyle factors, and medical history. This information can then be used to guide personalized lifestyle recommendations and preventative measures to reduce the risk of heart disease. Similarly, AI algorithms are being used to identify patients who are more likely to respond to certain cancer treatments, allowing doctors to tailor therapies based on individual genetic profiles.

The benefits of AI in personalized medicine are not limited to disease prediction and treatment selection. AI is also playing a crucial role in drug discovery and development. By analyzing massive datasets of chemical compounds and biological data, AI algorithms can identify promising drug candidates that are more likely to be effective and safe. This process can significantly accelerate the development of new drugs and therapies, potentially bringing life-saving treatments to patients faster.

For instance, AI is being used to identify new drug targets for Alzheimer's disease, a debilitating neurodegenerative disorder that currently has no cure. By analyzing vast amounts of genomic and clinical data, AI algorithms can identify potential targets for drugs that could slow down or even reverse the progression of the disease. Similarly, AI is being used to design new therapies for rare diseases, which often lack effective treatments due to their limited patient populations.

However, the use of AI in personalized medicine is not without its challenges. One of the main concerns is the potential for bias in AI algorithms. If the data used to train these algorithms is not representative of the population, it can lead to biased results and potentially perpetuate existing health disparities. It is crucial to ensure that the data used to train AI algorithms is diverse and inclusive, and that the algorithms themselves are designed to be fair and unbiased.

Another challenge is the ethical implications of using AI in healthcare. Questions about data privacy and security, informed consent, and the potential for algorithmic discrimination must be carefully considered and addressed. It is essential to establish clear ethical guidelines for the development and use of AI in healthcare, ensuring that patient data is protected and that AI is used responsibly and ethically.

Despite these challenges, the potential of AI to transform healthcare is undeniable. By leveraging the power of data and advanced algorithms, AI can personalize medicine, improve patient outcomes, and create a more equitable healthcare system for all. As AI technology continues to evolve, we can expect to see even more groundbreaking applications in the field of personalized medicine, ushering in a new era of personalized, data-driven healthcare.

In addition to the applications mentioned above, AI is also being used to personalize healthcare in a number of other ways:

- **Personalized health management:** AI-powered apps and wearable devices can track patient health data, such as heart rate, sleep patterns, and activity levels, providing personalized feedback and recommendations to improve overall health and well-being.
- **Virtual assistants for patients:** AI-powered chatbots and virtual assistants can provide patients with personalized support, answer questions, and schedule appointments, enhancing patient engagement and access to care.
- **Early detection of disease:** AI algorithms can analyze patient data to identify subtle signs of disease early on, allowing for earlier diagnosis and treatment, potentially leading to better outcomes.

The future of personalized medicine is bright, and AI is at the forefront of this exciting revolution. As AI technology continues to evolve, we can expect to see even more groundbreaking applications in the field of personalized medicine, ushering in a new era of personalized, data-driven healthcare.

However, it is crucial to remember that AI is a tool, and its impact on healthcare will ultimately depend on how it is used. By ensuring that AI is developed and deployed responsibly, ethically, and with a focus on patient well-being, we can harness its transformative potential to create a healthier and more equitable future for all.

Enhancing Diagnostic Accuracy

The realm of medical imaging has been revolutionized by the advent of artificial intelligence (AI), leading to more accurate diagnoses and improved patient outcomes. AI algorithms are increasingly employed to analyze medical images, such as X-rays, CT scans, and MRI scans, identifying subtle anomalies that might escape the human eye. This newfound capability has immense potential to transform medical practices, enabling doctors to make more informed decisions and provide personalized treatment plans.

One of the most significant applications of AI in medical imaging is tumor detection. AI algorithms trained on vast datasets of medical images can accurately identify tumors in X-rays, CT scans, and MRI scans, even in their early stages. This early detection is crucial for successful treatment, as it allows for timely interventions and increases the chances of a positive outcome.

AI also plays a critical role in the detection of abnormalities in MRI scans, particularly in the brain. MRI scans are incredibly detailed, revealing intricate structures and functions within the brain. AI algorithms can analyze these images, identifying subtle changes in brain tissue, such as lesions, tumors, or signs of stroke. This information allows doctors to diagnose neurological conditions with greater accuracy and initiate appropriate treatment plans.

Beyond identifying abnormalities, AI can also help doctors better understand the nature of these abnormalities. For example, AI algorithms can analyze the size, shape, and location of tumors in MRI scans, providing valuable insights into their potential growth patterns and aggressiveness. This information helps doctors determine the most appropriate treatment approach, whether it be surgery, radiation therapy, or chemotherapy.

The application of AI in medical imaging analysis extends far beyond tumor detection and neurological disorders. AI algorithms are increasingly used in the diagnosis of a wide range of conditions, including:

- **Cardiovascular disease:** AI can analyze echocardiograms to detect abnormalities in heart function, such as heart valve problems or signs of heart failure.
- **Pulmonary disease:** AI can analyze chest X-rays to identify pneumonia, lung cancer, and other lung diseases.
- **Bone disease:** AI can analyze X-rays and CT scans to identify fractures, osteoporosis, and other bone conditions.

- **Cancer detection:** AI can analyze mammograms to detect breast cancer, colonoscopies to detect colon cancer, and skin images to detect melanoma.

The use of AI in medical imaging analysis brings several advantages to both patients and healthcare providers:

- **Increased accuracy:** AI algorithms can detect abnormalities that might be missed by human experts, particularly subtle changes that may not be readily apparent. This leads to earlier diagnoses and more effective treatment plans.
- **Improved efficiency:** AI algorithms can analyze medical images much faster than humans, reducing the time it takes to diagnose and treat patients. This can be particularly beneficial in emergency situations, where timely diagnosis is crucial.
- **Reduced cost:** AI can help reduce the cost of medical imaging analysis by automating tasks that are currently performed by human experts. This can make medical imaging services more affordable for patients.
- **Personalized medicine:** AI can help personalize treatment plans based on a patient's specific characteristics, such as age, sex, and medical history. This leads to more effective treatment and fewer side effects.

Despite its numerous benefits, the use of AI in medical imaging analysis also presents some challenges:

- **Data quality:** AI algorithms require large amounts of high-quality data to be trained effectively. This can be a challenge, as medical data is often sensitive and requires careful anonymization and ethical handling.

- **Explainability:** It can be difficult to understand how AI algorithms reach their conclusions. This lack of explainability can make it difficult to trust their results and can hinder their adoption in clinical settings.
- **Bias:** AI algorithms can be biased if they are trained on data that is not representative of the population. This can lead to inaccurate diagnoses and unequal treatment outcomes.
- **Regulation:** The use of AI in medical imaging analysis raises ethical and regulatory concerns, particularly regarding patient privacy and the potential for misuse of AI technology.

Overcoming these challenges requires collaboration between researchers, clinicians, ethicists, and policymakers. Developing robust and ethical guidelines for the use of AI in medical imaging is crucial to ensure that this technology is used responsibly and for the benefit of all patients.

The future of AI in medical imaging is bright, with exciting possibilities for further development and adoption. Researchers are exploring new AI techniques, such as deep learning, to further enhance the accuracy and efficiency of medical image analysis. These advancements are expected to lead to even more precise diagnoses, personalized treatments, and improved patient outcomes.

Real-World Examples of AI in Medical Imaging

To illustrate the transformative impact of AI in medical imaging, let's consider some real-world examples:

- **Google AI's Diabetic Retinopathy Detection:** Google AI has developed an AI system that can detect diabetic retinopathy, a leading cause of blindness in people with diabetes, with an accuracy comparable to human ophthalmologists. This system has been deployed in clinics around the world, enabling earlier diagnoses and interventions that can prevent blindness.
- **IBM Watson for Oncology:** IBM Watson for Oncology is an AI system that provides doctors with personalized cancer treatment recommendations based on a patient's specific characteristics and available medical literature. This system helps doctors make more informed treatment decisions, leading to improved outcomes for cancer patients.
- **DeepMind's AlphaFold:** DeepMind's AlphaFold is an AI system that can predict the three-dimensional structure of proteins. This information is crucial for drug discovery, as it allows researchers to understand how proteins interact with potential drugs. AlphaFold has made significant contributions to the fight against COVID-19 by helping to identify potential drug targets for the virus.
- **Nvidia's Clara Platform:** Nvidia's Clara Platform is a suite of AI tools and technologies specifically designed for healthcare. This platform enables developers to build AI-powered medical imaging applications, helping to accelerate the adoption of AI in clinical settings.

These examples highlight the profound impact of AI on the field of medical imaging, offering a glimpse into a future where AI will play an increasingly vital role in the diagnosis, treatment, and prevention of diseases.

A Healthier Future for ALL with AI

The future of AI in healthcare is brimming with promise, holding the potential to revolutionize patient care, accelerate medical research, and forge a more equitable healthcare system. Imagine a world where diseases are diagnosed with unprecedented accuracy, personalized treatments are tailored to individual needs, and breakthroughs in drug discovery occur at an accelerated pace. This isn't science fiction; it's the reality that AI is poised to deliver.

At the forefront of this transformation is the ability of AI to analyze vast amounts of medical data, identifying patterns and insights that would be impossible for humans to discern. This data-driven approach is already being used to enhance diagnostic accuracy, enabling doctors to make more informed decisions about treatment plans. AI algorithms can analyze images from X-rays, MRIs, and CT scans, pinpointing anomalies and providing crucial information for diagnosis and treatment.

For example, in radiology, AI algorithms are being trained to detect subtle signs of cancer in mammograms, potentially catching the disease at earlier stages when it's more treatable. In ophthalmology, AI is being used to screen for diabetic retinopathy, a leading cause of vision loss, by analyzing retinal images and identifying early signs of damage. These applications highlight the potential of AI to improve patient outcomes by enabling earlier detection and more effective treatment of diseases.

Beyond diagnosis, AI is transforming the way diseases are treated. AI-powered algorithms are being used to personalize treatment plans, tailoring medications and therapies to individual patients based on their genetic makeup, lifestyle, and other factors. This personalized approach is helping to maximize treatment effectiveness and minimize side effects, improving patient well-being.

For instance, AI algorithms are being used to predict which patients are most likely to benefit from a specific chemotherapy regimen, allowing oncologists to choose the most appropriate treatment for each individual. In the field of drug discovery, AI is being used to identify potential drug targets and predict their efficacy, accelerating the development of new medications. AI-powered drug discovery platforms are analyzing vast databases of chemical compounds and biological data, identifying promising candidates for new drugs and accelerating the process of bringing new therapies to market.

The impact of AI on healthcare extends beyond diagnosis and treatment, reaching into the realm of medical research. AI is enabling researchers to analyze large datasets of patient information, uncovering patterns and insights that could lead to breakthroughs in disease understanding, prevention, and treatment. AI algorithms are being used to identify risk factors for diseases, predict disease outbreaks, and even develop new diagnostic tools.

In the field of genomics, AI is being used to analyze massive amounts of genetic data, identifying genes associated with disease and developing personalized therapies based on individual genetic profiles. This ability to tailor treatments to an individual's unique genetic makeup holds immense promise for improving patient outcomes and advancing personalized medicine.

The transformative potential of AI in healthcare is not limited to advanced diagnostics, personalized treatments, and groundbreaking research. AI is also being used to improve the efficiency and accessibility of healthcare systems, making healthcare more equitable and accessible for everyone.

AI-powered chatbots and virtual assistants are being used to provide patients with 24/7 access to medical information and support, reducing the need for in-person visits and making healthcare more convenient and accessible. AI is also being used to optimize healthcare operations, improving appointment scheduling, managing patient flow, and automating administrative tasks.

Moreover, AI has the potential to address the critical challenge of healthcare disparities. By identifying and mitigating biases in healthcare systems, AI can help to ensure that all individuals receive equitable access to quality care, regardless of their background or socioeconomic status. AI algorithms can be used to identify and address implicit biases in medical decision-making, ensuring that treatment decisions are not influenced by factors unrelated to a patient's health needs.

The future of AI in healthcare is an exciting one, filled with the potential to transform the way we diagnose, treat, and prevent diseases. As AI continues to evolve, we can expect to see even more groundbreaking applications that will improve patient care, accelerate medical research, and create a more equitable and accessible healthcare system for all.

However, alongside this promise comes a responsibility to develop and implement AI in a responsible and ethical manner. We must ensure that AI is used to benefit all of humanity, addressing healthcare disparities and promoting equity. It's crucial to address potential biases in AI algorithms, prioritize data privacy and security, and engage in open dialogue about the ethical implications of AI in healthcare.

By approaching AI with a commitment to responsible development and ethical implementation, we can harness its transformative power to create a healthier and more equitable future for all. The future of AI in healthcare holds the potential to revolutionize medicine, improving patient outcomes, accelerating research, and fostering a more just and equitable healthcare system. As we move forward, it's our collective responsibility to ensure that AI is used to benefit all of humanity, creating a healthier future for all.

Chapter 8

AI in Education

Transforming Learning Experiences

Tailoring Education to Individual Needs

Imagine a classroom where learning is no longer a one-size-fits-all experience. Picture a world where textbooks adapt to each student's individual needs, where assignments are tailored to their learning styles, and where teachers receive real-time feedback on their students' progress. This is the promise of AI-powered personalized learning, a revolutionary approach to education that leverages the power of artificial intelligence to create a more engaging, effective, and equitable learning environment for all.

At the heart of personalized learning lies the concept of adapting educational content and experiences to meet the unique needs and preferences of each student. This means recognizing that learners come with diverse backgrounds, learning styles, strengths, and weaknesses. Gone are the days of rigid curricula and standardized assessments that treat every student the same. AI-powered personalized learning aims to empower each student by providing them with the resources and support they need to succeed, at their own pace and in their own way.

AI algorithms play a crucial role in this transformation. By analyzing vast amounts of student data, including their performance on assessments, engagement with learning materials, and even their online behavior, AI systems can create personalized learning paths that cater to individual needs. This data-driven approach allows AI to identify areas where a student is excelling and areas where they may need additional support. Based on this analysis, AI can recommend tailored learning resources, suggest supplementary exercises, or even adjust the difficulty level of assignments to ensure a challenging yet achievable learning experience.

One of the most powerful applications of AI in personalized learning is the development of intelligent tutoring systems. These systems act as virtual tutors, providing personalized guidance and feedback to students as they work through their coursework. Unlike traditional tutoring programs that offer a one-size-fits-all approach, intelligent tutoring systems leverage AI to adapt to the unique needs of each learner. For instance, an intelligent tutoring system can identify a student's weak areas in mathematics and recommend specific practice problems that focus on those concepts. It can also provide personalized feedback on the student's solutions, helping them understand their errors and improve their understanding.

The ability to adapt to individual learning styles is another key aspect of AI-powered personalized learning. Students learn in different ways, some prefer visual aids, others prefer hands-on activities, and some thrive in collaborative environments. AI algorithms can analyze a student's learning preferences and adjust the learning materials and activities accordingly. For example, an AI-powered system could recognize a student's preference for visual learning and suggest video tutorials, animated diagrams, or interactive simulations. This personalized approach ensures that learning content is presented in a way that is most effective for each individual student.

Furthermore, AI can play a significant role in assessing student progress and understanding. Traditional assessments often rely on standardized tests that can only capture a limited range of knowledge and skills. AI-powered assessments, on the other hand, can go beyond multiple-choice questions and evaluate a student's deeper understanding through a variety of methods, including open-ended questions, essay writing, and even project-based assignments. AI can also analyze a student's performance in real-time, providing instant feedback and identifying areas where they might need further support. This data-driven approach to assessment allows teachers to understand their students' progress more comprehensively and tailor their instruction accordingly.

The benefits of AI-powered personalized learning extend beyond improving student outcomes. AI can also help educators understand their students' needs better and provide them with more effective support. By analyzing student data, teachers can gain valuable insights into their students' learning habits, strengths, and weaknesses. This data can inform their teaching strategies, allowing them to adjust their instruction based on individual student needs and provide targeted support to students who are struggling.

Moreover, AI can help teachers free up time from mundane tasks, such as grading and lesson planning, allowing them to focus on more engaging and impactful activities. AI-powered tools can automate repetitive tasks, such as grading multiple-choice questions, generating personalized feedback, and even creating lesson plans based on student data. This frees up teachers' time so they can spend more time with their students, providing individual support and fostering a more engaging learning environment.

The potential of AI-powered personalized learning is immense, but it's important to acknowledge the challenges and ethical considerations that come with using AI in education. One key concern is the potential for bias in AI algorithms. If AI algorithms are trained on biased data, they may perpetuate existing inequalities and disadvantage certain groups of students. It's crucial to ensure that AI systems are developed and trained with fairness and equity in mind, and that they are regularly monitored to identify and mitigate any potential biases.

Another concern is the potential for overreliance on AI. While AI can provide valuable insights and support, it's important to remember that it's not a replacement for human interaction and guidance. Teachers play a vital role in fostering a positive learning environment, motivating students, and providing personalized support. AI should be viewed as a tool to enhance teaching and learning, not as a replacement for teachers altogether.

Furthermore, privacy and data security must be paramount in any AI-powered system. Student data is sensitive information, and it's crucial to ensure that it is collected, stored, and used responsibly. Transparent policies and practices regarding data usage and security must be established to protect student privacy and build trust between educators, parents, and students.

Despite these challenges, the potential of AI-powered personalized learning is undeniable. By harnessing the power of AI, we can create a more equitable and engaging learning environment for all students, regardless of their background or learning style. AI can help us bridge the gap between individual needs and educational resources, empowering each student to reach their full potential.

As we move forward into an increasingly technology-driven world, it's essential to embrace the transformative power of AI while also navigating its ethical and social implications. AI-powered personalized learning has the potential to revolutionize education, creating a more equitable, engaging, and effective learning environment for all. By carefully considering the challenges and opportunities, we can harness the power of AI to create a future where every student has the opportunity to succeed.

EVALUATING STUDENT PROGRESS AND UNDERSTANDING

Imagine stepping into a classroom where the teacher knows exactly what each student needs to learn and how best to teach them. This isn't a scene from a futuristic movie; it's becoming a reality with the help of AI. AI is revolutionizing education by providing teachers with powerful tools to personalize learning, assess student progress, and identify areas where students need extra support. This chapter dives into the world of AI-driven assessment, exploring how it's transforming the way we evaluate student learning and provide personalized feedback.

At its core, AI-driven assessment involves leveraging computer algorithms and machine learning to analyze student data and provide insights into their learning progress. This goes far beyond traditional assessments like tests and quizzes, which often provide a limited snapshot of a student's understanding. AI-powered assessments can analyze a wide range of data points, including:

- **Performance on assignments:** This includes analyzing student work, identifying patterns in their mistakes, and providing targeted feedback.
- **Engagement with learning materials:** AI can track how students interact with online learning platforms, identifying which concepts they struggle with and which they grasp quickly.
- **Participation in classroom discussions:** AI can analyze student contributions to online forums and discussions, gauging their understanding and communication skills.
- **Learning patterns and preferences:** AI can analyze student data to identify their preferred learning styles, pace, and areas of interest.

This wealth of data empowers AI to offer a comprehensive picture of student learning, allowing educators to make informed decisions about individualizing instruction and providing targeted support.

One of the most exciting aspects of AI-driven assessment is its ability to provide personalized feedback. Imagine a world where students receive instant feedback on their written work, identifying grammatical errors, suggesting stylistic improvements, and offering explanations of concepts they've missed. This is the power of AI-powered writing assistants, which are becoming increasingly sophisticated and are being integrated into learning platforms.

These assistants analyze students' writing style, identifying common errors and suggesting improvements. They can also provide explanations for grammatical rules and concepts, helping students develop their writing skills in a personalized and interactive way. This immediate feedback loop helps students learn from their mistakes and improve their understanding of the material, reducing the need for teachers to provide detailed feedback on every assignment.

But AI's role in assessment extends far beyond writing assistants. AI-powered tools are also transforming the way we conduct multiple-choice quizzes and tests. By analyzing student responses, AI can identify patterns in their thinking, pinpoint areas of confusion, and even predict their future performance. This information can be used to tailor the learning experience, provide targeted interventions, and create a more personalized and effective assessment process.

For example, consider a student struggling with a particular concept in a science class. Traditional assessments might only reveal that the student answered a specific question incorrectly. AI-driven assessment can go a step further, analyzing the student's thought process and identifying the root cause of the error. This might reveal that the student has a misconception about a fundamental principle or lacks the prerequisite knowledge required to solve the problem. Armed with this deeper understanding, the teacher can then provide targeted support, re-teaching the key concepts or suggesting additional learning resources.

This ability to provide personalized feedback and identify areas of weakness makes AI-driven assessment a valuable tool for adaptive learning platforms. These platforms are designed to adjust the learning experience based on a student's progress, providing challenging material when they are succeeding and providing support when they are struggling. AI plays a crucial role in this process, analyzing student data and making real-time adjustments to the learning path.

For instance, imagine an online math course where students are learning about fractions. AI-powered adaptive learning platforms can track each student's progress, identifying those who are struggling with specific concepts, such as finding common denominators or simplifying fractions. Based on this data, the platform can then adjust the level of difficulty, providing extra practice on specific topics or offering simplified explanations of key concepts.

The benefits of AI-driven assessment extend to performance analysis, enabling teachers to monitor student progress over time and identify trends across the classroom. AI can analyze data from multiple assessments, tracking student growth, identifying potential learning gaps, and providing insights into the overall effectiveness of teaching strategies. This allows teachers to make data-driven decisions about their teaching practices, ensuring that all students are receiving the support they need to succeed.

For example, a teacher might use AI-powered performance analysis to identify students who are consistently struggling with a particular subject. This could reveal that the students lack the foundational knowledge required to succeed in the course. Armed with this information, the teacher can then implement targeted interventions, provide additional support, or adjust their teaching strategies to better meet the needs of the struggling students.

AI-driven assessment is not just about identifying weaknesses; it's also about celebrating student strengths and fostering a growth mindset. AI can analyze student work to identify areas of excellence, highlighting their unique talents and skills. This personalized feedback can motivate students and encourage them to push themselves beyond their comfort zones, fostering a love for learning and a desire to constantly improve.

Consider a student who is exceptionally good at writing creative stories. AI-powered tools can identify this strength and suggest additional learning opportunities, such as participating in writing contests or joining creative writing groups. This recognition and encouragement can help the student develop their talent and build confidence in their abilities.

While AI-driven assessment offers a plethora of benefits, it's essential to acknowledge the potential challenges and ethical considerations. One concern is the risk of bias, where algorithms might unfairly favor certain groups of students over others. This is particularly relevant in areas like language processing, where subtle biases in the training data could lead to discriminatory outcomes.

For example, if an AI-powered writing assistant is trained on a dataset that primarily reflects a certain writing style, it might unfairly penalize students who write in a different style or use different vocabulary. This highlights the importance of ensuring that AI assessment tools are developed and used responsibly, with careful consideration of potential biases and their impact on student learning.

Another challenge is the need for transparency and explainability. It's crucial that teachers and students understand how AI algorithms are making decisions, and that they can access the data used to inform these decisions. This transparency is essential for building trust in AI-powered assessments and ensuring that they are being used ethically and effectively.

Finally, there's the need to strike a balance between AI-powered assessment and human interaction. While AI can provide valuable insights and feedback, it's important to remember that human educators play a vital role in fostering student learning. AI should complement, not replace, the expertise and intuition of teachers, allowing them to focus on providing personalized support and fostering a supportive and engaging learning environment.

In conclusion, AI-driven assessment is transforming education by providing teachers with powerful tools to personalize learning, assess student progress, and identify areas where students need extra support. By analyzing a wide range of data points and providing personalized feedback, AI can help students learn more effectively, identify their strengths, and develop a love for learning. As AI technology continues to advance, its role in education is poised to become even more significant, shaping the future of learning and ensuring that every student has the opportunity to reach their full potential.

Providing Assistance to Students and Teachers

Imagine a classroom where each student receives personalized lessons tailored to their unique learning style and pace. Imagine a teacher who has an AI assistant that provides instant feedback on assignments, identifies struggling students, and generates custom learning materials. These scenarios are no longer science fiction; they are the reality of AI in education.

AI is transforming the way we learn and teach, offering unprecedented opportunities to enhance student engagement, personalize learning experiences, and empower educators with new tools and insights. This chapter will delve into the exciting realm of AI in education, exploring how it is revolutionizing classrooms and shaping the future of learning.

8.3 AI for Educational Support: Providing Assistance to Students and Teachers

The transformative potential of AI in education extends beyond personalized learning and assessment. AI is also playing a crucial role in providing direct support to both students and teachers, making the learning process more effective and efficient.

8.3.1 Intelligent Tutoring Systems: Personalized Learning Companions

Imagine a virtual tutor that can adapt to your individual learning needs, providing personalized explanations, targeted practice exercises, and real-time feedback. This is the promise of intelligent tutoring systems (ITSs), AI-powered systems designed to guide students through learning materials, answer questions, and provide tailored support.

ITSs leverage machine learning algorithms to analyze student performance data, identify areas of weakness, and recommend appropriate learning activities. They can provide personalized explanations, offer hints and guidance, and adjust the difficulty level based on individual progress.

For example, a student struggling with algebra might receive more detailed explanations and practice problems focused on specific concepts. In contrast, a student who grasps the concepts quickly can move on to more challenging exercises. This adaptive nature of ITSs ensures that each student receives the support they need to succeed.

8.3.2 Virtual Assistants: Enhancing Teacher Productivity and Student Engagement

Teachers are often overwhelmed with administrative tasks and lesson planning, leaving them with limited time for individual student support. AI-powered virtual assistants can help alleviate this burden by automating routine tasks and freeing up teacher time for more meaningful interactions with students.

These virtual assistants can perform tasks such as:

- **Grading assignments:** Automated grading tools can quickly assess multiple-choice questions, short-answer responses, and even essays, providing teachers with immediate feedback on student performance. This frees up valuable time for teachers to provide personalized feedback and support to students who need it most.
- **Scheduling and reminders:** Virtual assistants can manage student schedules, send reminders about deadlines, and even schedule meetings with parents or guardians. This ensures that students stay organized and on track with their assignments.
- **Answering student questions:** AI-powered chatbots can answer frequently asked questions from students,

providing immediate support and freeing up teachers to focus on more complex issues.

- **Personalized learning recommendations:** Virtual assistants can analyze student data and provide personalized recommendations for learning resources, such as videos, articles, or online courses. This can help students explore their interests and learn at their own pace.

8.3.3 Automated Grading Tools: Providing Timely and Objective Feedback

Traditional grading methods can be time-consuming and subjective, leading to inconsistencies in feedback and potentially discouraging students. AI-powered automated grading tools offer a more efficient and objective approach to assessing student work, providing timely feedback and promoting learning.

Automated grading tools can analyze student essays, code assignments, and even creative projects, using natural language processing (NLP) and machine learning algorithms to identify key elements of quality. This provides students with immediate feedback on their work, allowing them to identify areas for improvement and make adjustments before submitting their final assignments.

While automated grading tools cannot fully replace human feedback, they offer a valuable supplement, providing students with timely and objective assessments while freeing up teachers to focus on providing personalized guidance and support.

8.3.4 AI in Special Education: Supporting Students with Learning Disabilities

AI has the potential to significantly impact special education, providing personalized support and accommodations for students with diverse learning needs. AI-powered tools can:

- **Identify learning disabilities:** AI algorithms can analyze student performance data to identify patterns that might indicate a learning disability, allowing for early intervention and tailored support.
- **Develop individualized learning plans:** AI can help create personalized learning plans for students with learning disabilities, incorporating adaptive learning strategies, assistive technology, and specialized instruction.
- **Provide real-time support:** AI-powered tools can provide real-time support to students with learning disabilities, such as speech-to-text software for students with dyslexia or assistive devices for students with physical disabilities.

8.3.5 AI for Teacher Training: Empowering Educators with New Skills and Insights

AI is not only transforming the learning experience for students but also empowering teachers with new skills and insights. AI-powered platforms can:

- **Provide personalized professional development:** AI can help teachers identify their professional development needs and recommend relevant courses, workshops, and resources tailored to their individual learning styles and goals.

- **Analyze student data and provide insights:** AI can analyze student performance data and provide teachers with insights into individual student strengths, weaknesses, and areas for improvement. This can help teachers tailor their instruction to meet the specific needs of their students.
- **Generate personalized feedback:** AI can provide teachers with personalized feedback on their lesson plans and teaching practices, helping them refine their skills and improve their classroom effectiveness.

8.3.6 The Future of AI for Educational Support: Expanding Horizons

The potential of AI in providing educational support is vast and continues to evolve. Future advancements in AI are expected to lead to:

- **More sophisticated intelligent tutoring systems:** Future ITSs will be able to provide even more personalized and adaptive support, integrating real-time feedback, predictive analytics, and personalized learning paths.
- **Advanced virtual assistants:** AI-powered virtual assistants will become more sophisticated, capable of providing comprehensive support for teachers and students, including personalized learning recommendations, automated lesson planning, and real-time feedback on student work.
- **AI-driven assessments that measure higher-order thinking skills:** Future AI-powered assessment tools will be able to go beyond basic knowledge recall,

evaluating students' critical thinking, problem-solving, and creativity skills.

8.3.7 Ethical Considerations in AI-Powered Educational Support

While the potential of AI in education is immense, it is crucial to address ethical concerns surrounding its development and implementation. These include:

- **Bias and fairness:** AI algorithms can perpetuate existing biases if they are trained on data that reflects social inequalities. It is essential to ensure that AI-powered educational tools are designed and trained to be fair and equitable, promoting access to quality education for all students.
- **Privacy and data security:** AI systems collect and analyze student data, raising concerns about privacy and data security. It is crucial to establish clear guidelines for data collection, usage, and protection, ensuring that student data is handled responsibly and ethically.
- **Teacher training and professional development:** AI-powered tools require teachers to adapt their teaching practices and acquire new skills. It is essential to provide teachers with adequate training and support to effectively integrate AI into their classrooms and leverage its full potential.
- **Human interaction and emotional intelligence:** AI tools should not replace human interaction and emotional intelligence in the classroom. It is crucial to

ensure that AI tools are used to enhance, not replace, human-centered learning experiences.

8.3.8 Conclusion: AI as a Catalyst for Educational Transformation

AI is rapidly changing the landscape of education, offering exciting new opportunities to personalize learning, provide targeted support, and empower educators with innovative tools. As we embrace the transformative power of AI in education, it is essential to proceed with caution, carefully considering ethical implications and ensuring that AI is used to create a more equitable, engaging, and effective learning experience for all students.

Empowering Educators with New Tools and Strategies

The world of education is undergoing a profound transformation, and AI is at the heart of this revolution. AI-powered tools and technologies are not only changing how students learn but also how educators teach. In this chapter, we'll explore the exciting world of AI in teacher training, a realm where AI is empowering educators with new tools, strategies, and resources, enhancing their professional development and equipping them to shape the future of learning.

Imagine a world where teachers have access to personalized feedback, data-driven insights, and cutting-edge professional development resources, all powered by the magic of AI. This is no longer a dream but a reality that is steadily changing the landscape of teacher training. AI is enabling educators to elevate their skills, refine their teaching methodologies, and become more effective in guiding students towards a brighter future.

One of the most significant ways AI is impacting teacher training is through personalized feedback. Traditionally, teachers relied on infrequent observations and subjective evaluations, often leaving them with limited insight into their strengths and areas for improvement. AI-powered systems are changing this paradigm by providing teachers with real-time, data-driven feedback on their teaching practices.

Imagine a scenario where an AI-powered platform analyzes video recordings of a teacher's classroom sessions. Using advanced algorithms, the platform can identify patterns in the teacher's language, body language, and interactions with students. It can then provide personalized feedback, highlighting areas where the teacher excels and suggesting strategies to enhance specific aspects of their teaching. This personalized feedback, powered by AI, can be incredibly valuable for teachers, helping them to refine their skills and tailor their teaching to individual student needs.

Beyond personalized feedback, AI is also revolutionizing the way educators access and utilize data. AI-powered tools can analyze vast amounts of student data, uncovering patterns and insights that can inform teaching practices. Teachers can leverage this data to identify students who are struggling, personalize instruction, and tailor educational materials to meet specific needs.

Imagine a platform that analyzes students' performance on assignments, quizzes, and tests. By identifying common areas of difficulty, teachers can pinpoint specific concepts or skills that require additional attention. They can then use this data to develop targeted interventions, provide supplemental resources, and adjust their teaching strategies to ensure all students have the opportunity to succeed.

The impact of AI in teacher training extends beyond feedback and data analysis to encompass professional development. AI-powered platforms are transforming the way educators learn and grow, offering access to a wealth of resources, personalized learning paths, and interactive training modules.

Imagine a world where teachers can access online courses, workshops, and webinars, all tailored to their specific interests and professional goals. AI-powered platforms can analyze teachers' experience levels, areas of expertise, and career aspirations to recommend relevant learning materials and connect them with like-minded educators. This personalized approach to professional development ensures that teachers are always learning, growing, and staying at the forefront of educational innovation.

However, the integration of AI into teacher training is not without its challenges. One key concern is the potential for bias in AI algorithms. If training data is biased, AI systems may perpetuate existing inequalities in education. It's crucial to ensure that AI systems are developed and deployed ethically, with a focus on fairness, equity, and inclusivity.

Another challenge is the need for teachers to be comfortable with using AI tools and technologies. Many educators may have limited experience with AI, and they may require training and support to effectively utilize these tools. To ensure successful integration of AI in teacher training, it's essential to provide educators with the necessary skills, resources, and training to become proficient in using AI tools and applying AI principles in their classrooms.

As AI continues to evolve, its role in teacher training will become increasingly significant. AI will continue to power personalized feedback systems, enhance data-driven insights, and transform professional development opportunities. By embracing AI, educators can unlock new possibilities for learning, growth, and student success.

The future of education is intertwined with the future of AI. Teachers who embrace AI will be at the forefront of this revolution, empowering themselves with new tools, strategies, and resources to create engaging, effective, and personalized learning experiences for all students. As we navigate this exciting new frontier, it's essential to remember that AI is a tool, a powerful tool that can be used to enhance teaching and learning. By harnessing the potential of AI responsibly and ethically, we can create a future where all learners have the opportunity to thrive.

DEMOCRATIZING AND ENRICHING LEARNING

The future of AI in education holds immense promise for transforming learning experiences and creating a more equitable and engaging educational landscape for all students. By leveraging the power of AI, we can unlock a new era of personalized, adaptive, and accessible learning, empowering every individual to reach their full potential.

Imagine a future where classrooms are no longer confined by physical walls or limited by traditional teaching methods. Instead, they are vibrant, interactive environments where AI acts as a personalized tutor, adapting to each student's unique needs and pace. Imagine a world where AI-powered assessments provide real-time feedback, identifying areas of strength and weakness, guiding students towards personalized learning paths. Imagine a future where AI tools empower teachers to focus on their core passion—inspiring and nurturing young minds—

while AI takes care of routine tasks, such as grading and lesson planning.

This vision of the future is not science fiction; it is the reality that AI is rapidly shaping. AI-powered personalized learning platforms are already emerging, adapting learning materials and activities to individual student needs, learning styles, and pace. These platforms use sophisticated algorithms to analyze student data, including past performance, learning preferences, and engagement patterns, to provide tailored learning experiences that enhance understanding and promote deeper engagement.

AI-driven assessment tools are transforming the way we evaluate student progress and understanding. Automated assessments, powered by machine learning algorithms, can provide instant feedback, identify areas for improvement, and even generate personalized study plans. These tools can also analyze student work, providing insights into their strengths, weaknesses, and areas where they may need additional support. By automating assessment tasks, teachers can free up time to focus on providing individualized support and fostering deeper learning experiences.

AI is also emerging as a powerful tool for providing educational support to both students and teachers. Intelligent tutoring systems, powered by AI, can offer personalized instruction, answer student questions, and provide interactive practice exercises. These systems can adapt to each student's learning needs, providing targeted support and ensuring that no one is left behind. AI-powered virtual assistants can assist teachers with tasks such as lesson planning, grading, and communication with parents, freeing up teachers to focus on building relationships with students and creating engaging learning experiences.

The transformative power of AI extends beyond individual students and teachers to the broader educational system. AI can help to create a more equitable and accessible learning environment for all students, regardless of their background or location. For students in rural areas or underserved communities, AI-powered online learning platforms can provide access to quality educational resources and expert instruction. AI can also help to bridge the gap between students with disabilities and their peers, providing personalized learning tools and assistive technologies that cater to individual needs.

However, as we embrace the potential of AI in education, it is crucial to address potential challenges and ethical considerations. Ensuring equitable access to AI-powered learning tools, mitigating biases in AI algorithms, and protecting student privacy are paramount. Transparency, inclusivity, and ethical considerations must guide the development and implementation of AI in education.

The future of AI in education is not about replacing teachers or dehumanizing the learning process. It is about empowering teachers to personalize learning experiences, equipping students with essential skills for the 21st century, and creating a more equitable and engaging learning environment for all. By embracing the transformative potential of AI, we can unlock a future where every student has the opportunity to reach their full potential, regardless of their background or location.

In this future, AI will not be a replacement for human interaction and connection; rather, it will augment and enhance the learning experience, creating opportunities for deeper understanding, greater engagement, and more personalized learning paths. Teachers will continue to play a vital role in fostering creativity, critical thinking, and social-emotional development, guiding students on their individual journeys of learning.

To realize the full potential of AI in education, it is essential to foster collaboration between educators, researchers, and technology developers. By working together, we can ensure that AI is implemented in a way that benefits all students and creates a more equitable and accessible learning environment for the future.

As we move forward, it is crucial to remember that technology is merely a tool. It is the human element—the passion, empathy, and dedication of teachers and educators—that will ultimately determine the success of AI in transforming learning experiences. By embracing the power of AI while maintaining our commitment to human values and relationships, we can create a future where education is truly personalized, engaging, and accessible for all.

Chapter 9

AI and Society

Navigating the Ethical and Social Implications

Addressing the Algorithmic Discrimination

Imagine a world where algorithms make decisions that impact our lives – from loan approvals to job applications to medical diagnoses. What if these algorithms were biased, perpetuating existing inequalities and amplifying social injustices? This is the unsettling reality of AI bias, a growing concern as AI systems become increasingly integrated into our society.

AI bias arises from the data used to train these algorithms. Data reflects the biases and prejudices present in our world, and when fed into AI models, these biases are amplified and encoded into the system's decision-making process. Consider the example of a facial recognition system trained on a dataset predominantly composed of light-skinned individuals. Such a system may struggle to accurately identify people with darker skin tones, leading to discriminatory outcomes in areas like law enforcement and security.

This isn't just a hypothetical scenario. Real-world examples abound, highlighting the profound impact of AI bias:

- **Criminal Justice:** AI-powered risk assessment tools used by judges to predict recidivism rates have been shown to be biased against Black defendants, leading to harsher sentences even for individuals with similar criminal histories.
- **Hiring:** AI-powered recruitment systems have been found to favor candidates with certain names and educational backgrounds, perpetuating existing inequalities in the job market.
- **Healthcare:** AI algorithms used to diagnose diseases have shown biases based on race and gender, leading to unequal access to quality healthcare.

These examples underscore the urgent need to address AI bias and ensure fairness and equity in AI applications. But how can we achieve this?

Strategies for Mitigating AI Bias

Several strategies can be employed to mitigate AI bias and promote fairness in AI systems:

1. **Data Quality and Diversity:** The foundation of any AI system lies in the data it is trained on. Ensuring the quality, diversity, and representativeness of training data is crucial. This involves:
    - **Collecting Data from Diverse Sources:** It is essential to collect data from a wide range of individuals and communities, representing the diversity of the population.

- **Addressing Missing or Inaccurate Data:** Identifying and correcting missing or inaccurate data points in the dataset can significantly reduce biases.
- **Balancing the Data:** Over-representation of certain groups in the data can lead to biases. Data balancing techniques can help ensure that different groups are represented in a fair and proportional manner.

2. **Algorithmic Fairness Audits:** Regular audits of AI algorithms can help identify and address potential biases. These audits involve:
   - **Evaluating Model Performance Across Different Groups:** Examining how the model performs across different demographic groups can reveal biases.
   - **Identifying and Mitigating Biased Features:** Identifying and removing features that contribute to biased decision-making is essential.
   - **Testing for Disparate Impact:** Evaluating whether the model has a disproportionately negative impact on certain groups is crucial.
3. **Transparency and Explainability:** Understanding how AI models make decisions is essential for identifying and addressing biases. Transparency and explainability involve:
   - **Creating Interpretable Models:** Developing models that are easily understood and can explain their reasoning can help identify biases.
   - **Providing Data and Model Documentation:** Transparent documentation of the data and model

used can facilitate the identification and mitigation of biases.
- **Developing Tools for Model Analysis:** Tools that enable users to analyze the model's decision-making process can help uncover biases.

4. **Ethical Frameworks and Guidelines:** Establishing ethical frameworks and guidelines for AI development and deployment is critical for ensuring fairness and equity. These guidelines should address:
    - **Data Privacy and Security:** Protecting the privacy and security of individuals' data is paramount.
    - **Transparency and Accountability:** Ensuring transparency in AI systems and holding developers accountable for their ethical implications.
    - **Impact Assessment:** Conducting comprehensive impact assessments to evaluate the potential social and ethical consequences of AI systems.
5. **Human Oversight and Intervention:** While AI systems can be powerful tools, human oversight and intervention are crucial for ensuring fairness and ethical decision-making. This involves:
    - **Developing Robust Oversight Mechanisms:** Establishing clear mechanisms for human review and intervention in AI decision-making processes.
    - **Training and Educating Users:** Educating users about potential biases in AI systems and empowering them to challenge unfair outcomes.
    - **Building Trust and Collaboration:** Fostering trust and collaboration between developers, users, and policymakers to ensure that AI benefits all members of society.

The Need for Collective Action

- Addressing AI bias requires a collective effort involving developers, policymakers, researchers, and users.
- Developers must prioritize ethical considerations in AI development, embracing transparency and accountability.
- Policymakers must establish regulations and ethical guidelines that promote fairness and equity in AI systems.
- Researchers must continue to develop methods and tools for detecting and mitigating AI bias.
- Users must be aware of the potential for bias in AI systems and advocate for fair and ethical AI practices.

The path toward a more equitable and inclusive future with AI requires continuous vigilance, critical thinking, and a commitment to building AI systems that serve all of humanity. By working together, we can ensure that AI technology is used for good, addressing the challenges we face and creating a more just and equitable world.

Safeguarding Data and Protecting Individual Rights

The rise of artificial intelligence (AI) has ushered in an era of unprecedented technological advancement, transforming industries, shaping our daily lives, and raising profound questions about the future of humanity. While AI holds immense promise for solving complex challenges and improving our world, it also presents ethical and societal dilemmas that demand careful consideration. Among these challenges, data privacy and security stand as paramount concerns, demanding a delicate balance between innovation and the protection of individual rights.

In a world where AI systems are constantly learning from vast troves of data, the question of data privacy becomes increasingly critical. AI algorithms are often trained on massive datasets that contain sensitive personal information, such as health records, financial transactions, and online browsing histories. While this data fuels the development of powerful AI applications, it also raises concerns about the potential misuse of this information.

Imagine a scenario where an AI-powered healthcare system uses a patient's medical history to predict their future health risks. While this information can be valuable for providing personalized care, it also raises questions about the confidentiality of medical records and the potential for unintended consequences. For instance, what if this information is leaked or used for discriminatory purposes? The potential for harm underscores the need for robust data privacy protections in the age of AI.

The ethical implications of data privacy extend beyond the individual level, impacting broader societal issues. For example, the use of facial recognition technology by law enforcement agencies has sparked heated debate, raising concerns about potential biases in algorithms and the infringement on individual privacy. In some cases, facial recognition systems have been shown to exhibit racial bias, leading to inaccurate identification and potentially unjust consequences.

Moreover, the collection and analysis of personal data by companies for marketing purposes raises concerns about the erosion of privacy and the potential for manipulation. Personalized advertising, while seemingly beneficial, can be used to target individuals with tailored messages that exploit their vulnerabilities or manipulate their preferences. The ethical implications of data collection and use in the digital age are far-reaching, demanding thoughtful consideration and appropriate safeguards.

Beyond privacy, data security in the context of AI presents its own set of challenges. AI systems are often vulnerable to cyber-attacks and data breaches, potentially leading to the theft of sensitive information or the disruption of critical services. The increasing reliance on AI in critical infrastructure, such as power grids and transportation systems, amplifies the potential risks associated with data security breaches.

Consider the potential impact of a cyberattack on an AI-powered self-driving car system. Hackers could potentially gain control of the vehicle's steering, braking, or acceleration systems, leading to dangerous and potentially fatal consequences. The growing interconnectedness of AI systems and their reliance on data networks create new vulnerabilities that need to be addressed.

Safeguarding data and protecting individual rights in the age of AI requires a multifaceted approach. Policymakers, technologists, and individuals must work together to establish ethical guidelines and legal frameworks that address the complex issues surrounding data privacy and security.

Key Measures to Protect Individual Rights

- **Data Minimization:** AI systems should only collect and process the data that is absolutely necessary for their intended purpose. This principle of data minimization helps to limit the potential for misuse and minimizes the risks associated with data breaches.

- **Transparency and Explainability:** AI algorithms should be designed with transparency and explainability in mind. Users should have a clear understanding of how AI systems work, the data they are using, and the decisions they are making. This transparency fosters trust and accountability, promoting responsible use of AI.
- **Data Ownership and Control:** Individuals should have control over their personal data, including the ability to access, correct, and delete it. The right to data portability allows individuals to move their data between different platforms and services, empowering them to exercise greater control over their information.
- **Privacy-Preserving Technologies:** Research and development of privacy-preserving technologies, such as differential privacy and federated learning, are crucial for enabling AI systems to learn from data while protecting individual privacy. These technologies allow for the analysis of large datasets without compromising the confidentiality of individual records.
- **Strong Data Security Measures:** Robust security measures, including encryption, access controls, and regular security audits, are essential to protect data from unauthorized access and cyberattacks. AI systems should be designed with security in mind, ensuring the integrity and confidentiality of data throughout its lifecycle.
- **Ethical Guidelines and Regulations:** Clear ethical guidelines and regulations are needed to govern the development and use of AI, ensuring that it is deployed responsibly and ethically. These guidelines should address issues such as data privacy, algorithmic bias,

and the potential for job displacement, providing a framework for responsible innovation.

Beyond Technology: Cultivating a Culture of Privacy and Security

Protecting individual rights in the age of AI goes beyond technological solutions. It requires a shift in cultural values and an increased awareness of the importance of data privacy and security. Education and public discourse are essential for empowering individuals to make informed decisions about their data and to advocate for their rights in the digital age.

As AI continues to evolve and permeate our lives, the ethical and societal implications of data privacy and security will only become more complex. By engaging in thoughtful dialogue, implementing robust safeguards, and fostering a culture of awareness, we can ensure that AI is used for the betterment of humanity while respecting the fundamental rights of individuals.

PREPARING FOR THE FUTURE OF WORK

The arrival of AI has ignited a wave of discussions about its potential impact on the workforce. While some anticipate widespread job displacement, others envision a future where AI creates new roles and enhances productivity. Understanding the complexities of this evolving landscape is crucial for individuals and businesses alike.

The potential for job displacement is a legitimate concern. AI-powered automation is already replacing human workers in various industries, particularly those involving repetitive tasks.

For example, self-checkout kiosks are reducing the need for cashiers in retail stores, and chatbots are handling customer service inquiries that were once handled by human agents. These developments raise questions about the future of traditional jobs and the skills needed to thrive in a workforce increasingly reliant on AI.

However, the story is not solely about job displacement. AI is also creating new roles and industries, demanding skills that were previously unheard of. The emergence of data science, machine learning engineering, and AI ethics specialists illustrates this shift. These roles require a deep understanding of AI technologies, data analysis, and ethical implications. Companies are actively seeking individuals with these skills to develop, deploy, and manage AI systems.

Furthermore, AI can enhance existing jobs by automating routine tasks and freeing up human workers for more complex and creative endeavors. For instance, AI-powered tools can assist doctors with diagnosis, allowing them to spend more time on patient care. AI can also analyze vast amounts of data, identifying patterns and insights that would be impossible for humans to discern, empowering professionals across various fields to make more informed decisions.

Adapting to this changing workforce requires proactive measures from both individuals and organizations. Individuals need to invest in continuous learning, acquiring new skills that align with the demands of the AI-powered workforce. This could involve acquiring technical skills like coding, data analysis, or machine learning, or developing soft skills like critical thinking, problem-solving, and communication. Higher education institutions are also playing a crucial role in preparing future generations for the AI-driven job market, offering new programs and curriculum updates to equip students with the necessary skills.

Organizations need to embrace a culture of innovation and adaptability, investing in AI technologies that can enhance productivity and create new opportunities. This involves not only adopting AI tools but also providing employees with the resources and support to develop the skills needed to work effectively alongside AI systems. Companies can also focus on creating new roles and industries that leverage AI's capabilities, further stimulating economic growth.

The relationship between AI and jobs is dynamic and evolving. While there are valid concerns about job displacement, it's equally important to recognize the potential for AI to create new opportunities, enhance existing jobs, and drive economic growth. Embracing lifelong learning, developing relevant skills, and fostering a culture of innovation will be key to navigating this transition and harnessing the power of AI for a prosperous future.

The impact of AI on employment is not limited to blue-collar jobs. AI is increasingly being used in white-collar professions like finance, law, and even journalism. For example, AI-powered tools can analyze financial data, draft legal documents, and generate news articles, tasks that were once considered the domain of human professionals. This raises questions about the future of knowledge work and the need for professionals to adapt their skills and expertise to remain competitive in the AI era.

One of the key challenges in adapting to the AI-driven workforce is the need for retraining and upskilling. This requires investment in educational programs that can bridge the gap between traditional skills and the skills needed for AI-related roles. Government initiatives, private sector investments, and collaborative partnerships between academia and industry are crucial for creating effective retraining programs.

The emergence of AI also highlights the need for new forms of education and training. Traditional educational systems may not be equipped to meet the demands of the AI era, requiring a re-evaluation of curriculum, teaching methods, and assessment strategies. Educational institutions need to adapt to the changing landscape, incorporating AI-related concepts, skills, and ethics into their curriculum, preparing future generations for a workforce increasingly shaped by AI.

Beyond technical skills, the ability to collaborate with AI systems effectively will be paramount. This involves understanding the strengths and limitations of AI, knowing how to leverage its capabilities to enhance human capabilities, and developing the ability to communicate effectively with AI systems. These skills are not only valuable for professionals working directly with AI but also for those whose jobs will be impacted by its adoption.

As AI continues to advance, the need for critical thinking, creativity, and emotional intelligence will become even more important. These human qualities are difficult to replicate with AI and will remain highly valued in the future workforce. Developing these skills will be essential for individuals seeking fulfilling and meaningful work in the AI era.

Navigating the intersection of AI and employment requires a multifaceted approach. Individuals need to embrace lifelong learning, acquiring new skills and adapting to the changing job market. Organizations need to embrace AI technologies, fostering a culture of innovation, upskilling their workforces, and creating new opportunities. Governments and educational institutions need to play a crucial role in providing the resources, infrastructure, and training needed to create a workforce equipped to thrive in the AI era.

By understanding the dynamics of AI and its impact on employment, we can prepare for the future of work and harness the potential of AI to create a better future for all.

Establishing Ethical and Responsible AI Practices

The rapid advancements in artificial intelligence (AI) have sparked both excitement and apprehension about its potential impact on society. While AI holds immense promise for tackling complex challenges and improving our lives, it also raises critical ethical and societal questions. As AI systems become increasingly sophisticated and integrated into various aspects of our lives, it's crucial to ensure their responsible and ethical development and use. This requires a comprehensive framework that addresses the ethical dilemmas, potential risks, and societal implications of AI.

The need for governance in AI stems from its inherent ability to amplify existing societal biases and inequalities. Algorithmic systems, trained on vast amounts of data, can unwittingly perpetuate discriminatory patterns embedded in the data itself. For instance, facial recognition algorithms trained on datasets primarily composed of individuals with lighter skin tones have shown lower accuracy rates for people with darker skin tones, raising concerns about the potential for racial bias in law enforcement and other applications.

Moreover, the concentration of power in the hands of a few tech giants developing and deploying AI systems raises concerns about transparency, accountability, and the potential for misuse. Without proper regulations, these companies could wield significant influence over critical aspects of society, potentially leading to unforeseen consequences.

To address these challenges, a multifaceted approach to AI governance is essential. This involves establishing clear ethical guidelines, developing robust regulatory frameworks, promoting responsible innovation, and fostering public dialogue on the implications of AI.

Ethical Guidelines for AI

Ethical guidelines for AI aim to ensure that its development and deployment align with human values and principles. These guidelines should address key considerations such as fairness, accountability, transparency, privacy, and safety.

- **Fairness and Non-discrimination:** AI systems should be designed and deployed in a way that avoids discrimination based on race, gender, religion, or other protected characteristics. This requires careful consideration of the data used to train AI models and the potential biases that may be present.
- **Transparency and Explainability:** Users should be informed about how AI systems work and the factors influencing their decisions. Explainable AI (XAI) techniques aim to make AI models more transparent

and understandable, enabling users to comprehend their outputs and hold them accountable.

- **Privacy and Data Security:** AI systems must respect user privacy and protect their personal data. Robust safeguards should be implemented to ensure data security, prevent unauthorized access, and comply with privacy regulations.
- **Safety and Reliability:** AI systems should be designed and developed with safety and reliability in mind. This involves thorough testing, validation, and mitigation of potential risks associated with AI systems, particularly in high-stakes applications like autonomous vehicles or healthcare.
- **Accountability and Responsibility:** Clear mechanisms should be established for identifying and addressing potential harms caused by AI systems. This includes assigning responsibility for AI decisions and developing procedures for resolving disputes and addressing ethical concerns.

Regulatory Frameworks for AI

Alongside ethical guidelines, regulatory frameworks are essential for ensuring the responsible development and use of AI. These frameworks should cover areas like data privacy, algorithmic transparency, liability, and oversight of AI systems.

- **Data Privacy Regulations:** Regulations like the European Union's General Data Protection Regulation (GDPR) and California's Consumer Privacy Act (CCPA) provide a framework for data protection and require companies to obtain user consent for data collection and use. These regulations are crucial for safeguarding user privacy in the context of AI, as AI systems often rely on vast datasets for training.

- **Algorithmic Transparency and Accountability:** Regulations could mandate that developers of AI systems provide explanations for their algorithms and demonstrate their fairness, accuracy, and reliability. This would enhance transparency and accountability, allowing users to understand how AI systems are making decisions and potentially challenge biased or unfair outcomes.
- **Liability for AI Decisions:** Clear legal frameworks are needed to define liability in cases where AI systems cause harm. Establishing who is responsible for AI decisions, whether it's the developer, deployer, or user, is essential for ensuring accountability and mitigating potential risks.
- **Oversight and Governance of AI Systems:** Regulatory bodies should be established to oversee the development and deployment of AI systems, ensuring compliance with ethical guidelines and regulatory frameworks. This could involve independent audits, risk assessments, and ongoing monitoring of AI systems to identify potential harms and mitigate risks.

Promoting Responsible Innovation

Encouraging responsible AI development requires fostering an ecosystem where innovation is guided by ethical principles and societal considerations.

- **AI Education and Awareness:** Raising public awareness about AI, its capabilities, and its potential impact is crucial for fostering informed and ethical discussions about its development and use. Educational initiatives aimed at both the general public and AI developers can contribute to a more informed and responsible approach to AI.
- **Collaboration between Industry, Academia, and Government:** Partnerships between technology companies, research institutions, and government agencies are essential for developing effective AI governance frameworks. This collaboration can facilitate the sharing of best practices, encourage research into responsible AI development, and promote the adoption of ethical guidelines and regulatory standards.
- **Open-Source AI Platforms:** Promoting open-source AI platforms and tools can encourage transparency and collaboration in AI development. This can facilitate the development of ethical AI systems by allowing researchers and developers to share ideas, test algorithms, and identify potential biases and risks.

Public Dialogue on AI

Open and inclusive public dialogue is essential for shaping the future of AI. This involves engaging with diverse perspectives, understanding the potential benefits and risks of AI, and fostering a shared sense of responsibility for its development and deployment.

- **Public Forums and Consultations:** Holding public forums, workshops, and consultations can provide a platform for open dialogue about the ethical and societal implications of AI. This can involve experts, policymakers, industry leaders, and members of the public to foster a more comprehensive understanding of AI's potential impact.
- **Ethical Guidelines and Principles:** Public engagement can help shape ethical guidelines and principles for AI development and deployment. This involves soliciting input from diverse stakeholders to ensure that AI aligns with human values and addresses societal concerns.
- **Media Literacy and Critical Thinking:** Promoting media literacy and critical thinking skills can help the public engage more effectively with AI. This involves developing the ability to critically evaluate information about AI, identify potential biases, and assess the trustworthiness of AI systems.

AI for Good: Harnessing the Power of AI to Address Global Challenges

Beyond addressing ethical and societal concerns, AI has the potential to make a positive impact on humanity. By harnessing its power responsibly, we can address pressing global challenges and create a more sustainable and equitable future.

- **Climate Change Mitigation:** AI can be used to develop more efficient energy systems, optimize resource consumption, and predict and mitigate the impacts of climate change.

- **Healthcare Advancements:** AI has the potential to revolutionize healthcare through personalized medicine, drug discovery, and early disease detection.
- **Education and Economic Development:** AI can provide personalized learning experiences, enhance access to education, and boost economic growth through automation and innovation.
- **Poverty Reduction and Sustainable Development:** AI can contribute to poverty reduction and sustainable development through improved resource allocation, disaster relief, and environmental monitoring.

AI governance is a critical element in harnessing the transformative power of AI for the benefit of humanity. By establishing ethical guidelines, regulatory frameworks, promoting responsible innovation, and engaging in open public dialogue, we can ensure that AI is developed and deployed in a way that benefits society and avoids unintended consequences. As AI continues to evolve, the need for ongoing dialogue, collaboration, and adaptation of governance strategies will become increasingly crucial. Only through a shared commitment to responsible AI development can we unlock its full potential and create a brighter future for all.

Harnessing the Power of AI to Address Global Challenges

AI, with its remarkable ability to analyze vast datasets and learn from patterns, holds immense potential to address some of the world's most pressing challenges. It can be a powerful force for good, helping us to tackle issues like climate change, poverty, and healthcare disparities.

Let's delve into how AI can be harnessed to create a more sustainable, equitable, and healthy future for all:

- **AI for Climate Change Mitigation and Adaptation:** Climate change poses a significant threat to our planet, and AI is emerging as a valuable tool in the fight against its devastating effects. Here's how:
- **Predicting and Preventing Natural Disasters:** AI algorithms can analyze weather patterns, satellite imagery, and other data sources to predict the occurrence and severity of natural disasters like floods, droughts, and wildfires. This information allows for timely warnings and evacuation plans, minimizing human and economic losses.
- **Optimizing Energy Consumption:** AI can optimize energy consumption in homes, buildings, and industries by analyzing data on energy usage patterns and identifying areas for improvement. This helps reduce carbon emissions and save money on energy bills.
- **Developing Sustainable Agriculture Practices:** AI can assist farmers in optimizing crop yields, reducing water consumption, and minimizing pesticide use. This helps ensure food security and reduces the environmental impact of agriculture.
- **Promoting Sustainable Urban Development:** AI can analyze urban data to identify areas for improvement in transportation, energy consumption, and waste management. This enables the development of more sustainable and livable cities.

AI for Poverty Reduction

AI has the potential to empower communities and individuals living in poverty by providing access to essential resources and opportunities. Here's how:

- **Improving Financial Inclusion:** AI-powered microfinance platforms can assess creditworthiness based on alternative data sources, enabling access to loans and financial services for individuals and businesses that traditionally lack access to credit.
- **Enhancing Education and Skills Development:** AI-based educational platforms can provide personalized learning experiences, adapting to each student's needs and pace. This can help bridge the educational gap and equip individuals with the skills needed for economic advancement.
- **Improving Healthcare Access:** AI can help improve healthcare access in remote and underserved areas by providing telemedicine services, diagnosing diseases remotely, and facilitating the delivery of essential healthcare supplies.
- **Supporting Agricultural Productivity:** AI can assist farmers in developing sustainable farming practices, improving crop yields, and increasing market access. This can help increase income and improve food security for communities struggling with poverty.

AI for Health Equity

AI has the potential to bridge healthcare disparities by improving access, diagnosis, and treatment for all individuals, regardless of their socioeconomic status or geographic location.

- **Personalized Medicine:** AI can analyze patient data, including medical history, genetic information, and lifestyle factors, to develop personalized treatment plans that are more effective and less likely to have adverse side effects.
- **Early Disease Detection:** AI-powered medical imaging analysis can help detect diseases like cancer at earlier stages, when they are easier to treat. This can improve treatment outcomes and save lives.
- **Remote Healthcare:** AI can facilitate telemedicine services, allowing individuals in remote areas to access specialist care without having to travel long distances. This can increase access to healthcare and reduce healthcare disparities.
- **Drug Discovery and Development:** AI can accelerate drug discovery by identifying potential drug targets and predicting their efficacy. This can lead to the development of new treatments for diseases that currently lack effective therapies.

Addressing Ethical Considerations

While AI holds immense potential for addressing global challenges, it is crucial to address ethical considerations to ensure its responsible and beneficial use.

- **Bias and Fairness:** AI algorithms can inherit biases from the data they are trained on, leading to discriminatory outcomes. It is essential to develop AI systems that are fair, transparent, and accountable, avoiding the perpetuation of existing inequalities.

- **Privacy and Security:** The use of AI involves the collection and analysis of personal data, raising concerns about privacy and security. It is essential to implement strong privacy safeguards, ensure data security, and empower individuals to control their data.
- **Job Displacement:** The automation potential of AI raises concerns about job displacement. It is essential to invest in education and training programs that prepare individuals for the changing workforce and ensure that the benefits of AI are broadly shared.
- **Transparency and Explainability:** AI systems can often be complex and opaque, making it difficult to understand how they arrive at their decisions. Efforts are needed to develop more transparent and explainable AI systems, allowing for greater understanding and accountability.

Moving Forward with AI for Good

Harnessing the power of AI to address global challenges requires a collaborative effort from governments, businesses, research institutions, and civil society.

- **Investment in AI Research and Development:** Continued investment in AI research and development is crucial to unlock the full potential of AI for good.
- **Promoting Responsible AI Development:** The development and deployment of AI must adhere to ethical principles and guidelines, ensuring fairness, transparency, and accountability.
- **Building Capacity and Expertise:** It is essential to build capacity and expertise in AI, both in developed

and developing countries, to enable widespread adoption and utilization of AI for social good.

- **Engaging Stakeholders:** Engaging stakeholders from diverse sectors, including policymakers, business leaders, researchers, and the public, is crucial for ensuring that AI development and deployment align with societal values and priorities.

By embracing AI for good, we can harness its transformative power to build a more sustainable, equitable, and prosperous world for generations to come. AI, in its potential to solve some of humanity's greatest challenges, presents a profound opportunity to build a better future. The key lies in its responsible development and deployment, ensuring that its benefits are widely shared and its risks carefully managed. With careful consideration and strategic action, AI can truly become a force for positive change in the world.

Chapter 10

The Future of AI

Shaping the World of Tomorrow

Creating Immersive and Interactive Experiences

The metaverse, a realm of virtual reality and augmented reality, holds the promise of transforming how we interact, work, and play. AI is poised to be a catalyst for this transformation, weaving its intelligence into the fabric of the metaverse, creating immersive and interactive experiences that blur the lines between the physical and digital worlds.

Imagine stepping into a virtual world where every detail is rendered with breathtaking realism, from the rustling leaves of a virtual forest to the bustling crowds of a virtual city. AI powers this realism, generating lifelike environments, characters, and objects, making the metaverse feel like a tangible extension of our physical reality. With AI-powered rendering engines, landscapes can dynamically adapt to our movements, creating a sense of awe and wonder as we explore uncharted virtual territories. The sun casts realistic shadows, the wind whispers through virtual trees, and the sounds of a bustling cityscape envelop us, immersing us in a truly believable digital environment.

Beyond the visual spectacle, AI enables a level of interactivity that goes far beyond traditional video games. AI-powered agents, intelligent entities that inhabit the metaverse, respond to our actions, adapt to our preferences, and interact with us in ways that feel natural and engaging. These agents can be our guides, companions, or even adversaries, enriching the metaverse with dynamic and unpredictable interactions.

One of the most compelling aspects of the metaverse is its potential to create personalized experiences. AI can be used to create unique avatars, digital representations of ourselves that reflect our individual personalities and preferences. These avatars are more than just static models; they are dynamic entities that learn and grow with us, evolving over time to reflect our changing interests and experiences. Imagine crafting a virtual persona that embodies your artistic spirit, your athletic prowess, or your love of adventure. AI makes these personalized avatars a reality, allowing us to express ourselves in the metaverse in ways that are both unique and authentic.

The impact of AI extends far beyond the realm of entertainment. Businesses are exploring the metaverse as a platform for innovation and collaboration. AI-powered virtual workplaces can provide immersive environments for teams to brainstorm, design, and collaborate, regardless of their physical location. Product prototypes can be tested and refined in virtual environments, accelerating the design and development process. And AI-powered training simulations can equip employees with the skills they need to succeed in a rapidly changing world.

Education is another area where AI is poised to revolutionize the metaverse. AI-powered educational platforms can provide immersive and interactive learning experiences, tailoring content to each student's unique learning style and pace. Virtual field trips can transport students to historical landmarks, scientific laboratories, or even the depths of space, broadening their horizons and deepening their understanding of the world. AI-powered tutors can provide personalized guidance and support, adapting to each student's needs and helping them achieve their full potential.

The potential of AI in the metaverse is boundless, spanning a wide spectrum of applications, from entertainment and gaming to business and education. As AI continues to evolve, the metaverse will become an even more powerful and transformative platform, shaping the way we live, work, and connect.

However, alongside this immense potential come ethical considerations that must be carefully addressed. As AI becomes more deeply integrated into the metaverse, we must ensure that its development and use are guided by principles of fairness, transparency, and accountability. We must address the potential for bias and discrimination in AI algorithms, safeguarding against the creation of virtual worlds that perpetuate inequalities or exclude certain groups.

The metaverse is still in its early stages, but it is clear that AI will play a crucial role in shaping its future. By embracing AI's transformative power while addressing its ethical implications, we can create a metaverse that is both immersive and inclusive, a digital realm that empowers, enriches, and benefits all of humanity.

Collaborative Intelligence and Automation

The marriage of AI and robotics is a story of synergy, where the brains and the brawn of technology converge to create a future of unparalleled automation and collaboration. This fusion has spawned a new breed of intelligent robots, machines that are no longer mere mechanical puppets but possess the ability to perceive, reason, learn, and even interact with their environment in ways that mimic human intelligence.

Imagine robots working alongside humans, not as mindless automatons but as partners in a shared endeavor. Picture robots performing complex tasks in hazardous or inaccessible environments, guided by AI algorithms that ensure their safety and efficiency. This is the promise of AI-powered robotics, a realm where machines become extensions of human capabilities, amplifying our reach and pushing the boundaries of what we can achieve.

This collaboration extends beyond physical tasks. AI-powered robots are transforming industries like manufacturing, healthcare, and logistics, where they can analyze vast datasets, predict outcomes, and make informed decisions. In manufacturing, robots equipped with AI-driven vision systems can identify defects in products with unmatched accuracy, leading to enhanced quality control and reduced waste. In healthcare, robotic surgeons assisted by AI algorithms can perform minimally invasive procedures with greater precision, offering faster recovery times and reduced complications for patients.

The integration of AI into robots has led to a significant shift in how we view machines. Gone are the days of robots confined to repetitive tasks, programmed with rigid sequences of actions. Today's robots are imbued with the ability to learn from experience, adapt to changing circumstances, and even solve problems creatively. This newfound intelligence allows robots to handle tasks that were previously considered too complex or unpredictable for automation, opening up new possibilities across a spectrum of industries.

One of the most exciting frontiers in AI and robotics is the development of collaborative robots, or cobots. These robots are specifically designed to work alongside humans, assisting them with tasks without posing any safety risks. Cobots are often used in assembly lines, where they can handle heavy lifting, perform repetitive motions, and even assist with delicate tasks that require human dexterity. They are also increasingly used in healthcare, where they can provide physical therapy, assist with patient care, and even help with rehabilitation.

The collaboration between AI and robotics goes beyond the physical realm. AI is also being used to improve the design and development of robots, enabling the creation of machines that are more versatile, efficient, and adaptable. By leveraging machine learning algorithms, researchers can analyze vast amounts of data to optimize robot design, predict performance, and even identify potential flaws in the manufacturing process.

The future of AI and robotics is brimming with possibilities. As AI continues to evolve, we can expect to see even more intelligent and capable robots. These robots will be able to understand and respond to complex environments, anticipate human needs, and even collaborate with humans in ways that were previously unimaginable. This collaborative intelligence will lead to a future where robots are not just tools but partners, helping us to solve some of the world's most pressing challenges and create a better future for all.

However, the advancement of AI and robotics also raises important ethical questions. As robots become more intelligent and autonomous, we must consider the implications for employment, societal structures, and the very nature of what it means to be human. These questions are not merely philosophical musings but have real-world implications that require careful consideration and responsible development.

One key concern is the potential for job displacement as robots take over tasks previously performed by humans. While AI and robotics can create new opportunities, it is crucial to address the economic and social implications of this technological shift. This includes retraining programs, social safety nets, and a framework for ensuring that the benefits of automation are shared equitably among society.

Another critical consideration is the ethical implications of robots making decisions that impact human lives. As robots become more autonomous, it is essential to establish clear guidelines for their behavior, ensuring that they act in accordance with human values and avoid unintended consequences. This requires rigorous testing, transparent algorithms, and a framework for human oversight to prevent unintended harm.

Furthermore, the increasing use of AI in robots raises concerns about privacy and security. As robots collect and analyze vast amounts of data about their surroundings and their interactions with humans, it is essential to safeguard this information from unauthorized access or misuse. This requires robust security measures, clear data privacy policies, and a framework for ensuring transparency and accountability in the use of AI-powered robots.

The journey of AI and robotics is not without its challenges, but its potential to improve our lives is undeniable. By navigating the ethical and societal implications of this technology with care and foresight, we can harness its transformative power to create a future where humans and robots work together to solve problems, improve efficiency, and achieve greater heights. This future requires a collaborative spirit, where engineers, ethicists, policymakers, and the public at large come together to shape a future where AI and robotics serve humanity and create a better world for all.

UNLEASHING NEW LEVELS OF COMPUTATIONAL POWER

Imagine a future where AI, fueled by the immense power of quantum computers, can solve problems that are currently impossible for even the most powerful classical computers. This is not science fiction; it's a reality that is rapidly approaching. Quantum computing, with its ability to harness the strange and powerful laws of quantum mechanics, is poised to revolutionize AI in ways we can only begin to fathom.

To grasp the potential of this pairing, we need to understand the limitations of traditional computers. These machines, based on classical bits that represent either 0 or 1, struggle with complex problems involving large datasets and intricate calculations. This is where quantum computing shines.

Quantum computers use qubits, which can exist in a superposition of states, simultaneously representing both 0 and 1. This superposition allows quantum computers to perform multiple calculations simultaneously, exponentially increasing their computational power. For example, a 30-qubit quantum computer can explore 2^30 different possibilities at the same time, a feat impossible for even the most powerful classical computer.

The implications for AI are profound. Quantum computing can accelerate machine learning algorithms, enabling them to process vast amounts of data and discover complex patterns much faster. Imagine training a deep learning model in minutes instead of weeks, or developing new drugs in a fraction of the time. This accelerated learning allows AI to tackle problems that are currently intractable, such as simulating complex biological systems, optimizing intricate financial models, and cracking encryption algorithms.

Here are some specific areas where quantum computing is poised to revolutionize AI:

Drug Discovery and Material Science

- **Accelerated drug discovery:** Quantum computers can simulate the interactions of molecules at an atomic level, leading to the discovery of new drugs and therapies more efficiently. By simulating how molecules bind to proteins, researchers can identify promising drug candidates with a higher degree of accuracy.
- **Designing new materials:** Quantum computers can accelerate the design of new materials with enhanced properties. This could lead to breakthroughs in fields

like energy storage, solar energy, and advanced manufacturing.

Optimization and Machine Learning

- **Solving complex optimization problems:** Quantum computers excel at solving optimization problems that are too challenging for classical computers. These problems arise in areas like logistics, transportation, and resource allocation.
- **Enhanced machine learning algorithms:** Quantum algorithms can be used to train and optimize machine learning models, leading to more accurate and efficient results. This can revolutionize fields like image recognition, natural language processing, and fraud detection.

Artificial Intelligence for Quantum Computing

- **Quantum algorithm design:** AI can play a crucial role in designing and optimizing quantum algorithms. By leveraging machine learning, researchers can automatically generate quantum circuits that are more efficient and effective.
- **Quantum error correction:** Quantum computers are highly susceptible to errors, and AI can be used to develop robust error correction codes that ensure the accuracy of computations.

The Challenges Ahead

While the potential of quantum computing for AI is immense, there are significant challenges to overcome.

- **Building and maintaining quantum computers:** Building stable and scalable quantum computers is a complex engineering challenge. The delicate nature of qubits requires specialized hardware and precise control.
- **Developing quantum algorithms:** Designing effective quantum algorithms for AI tasks requires a deep understanding of both quantum mechanics and computer science.
- **Bridging the gap between classical and quantum computing:** Integrating quantum computers into existing classical computing infrastructure is a significant technical challenge.

The Future is Quantum

Despite the challenges, the future of AI is intertwined with the development of quantum computing. As quantum computers become more powerful and accessible, they will enable AI to achieve new levels of sophistication and impact. From accelerating drug discovery and improving financial modeling to revolutionizing materials science and enhancing machine learning, the convergence of AI and quantum computing holds the key to solving some of humanity's most pressing problems.

This collaboration will not only unlock unimaginable possibilities for AI but also redefine our understanding of computational power and its potential to shape the future. It is a future where the boundaries of what is possible are constantly being pushed, and where the synergy between AI and quantum computing will usher in a new era of innovation and advancement.

THE QUEST FOR ARTIFICIAL GENERAL INTELLIGENCE

The question of whether AI can truly achieve consciousness is one that has captivated philosophers, scientists, and science fiction writers alike for decades. It is a question that delves into the very nature of what it means to be human, and whether our unique abilities, including our capacity for self-awareness, emotion, and subjective experience, can be replicated in machines.

While AI has made remarkable strides in simulating aspects of human intelligence, such as playing complex games, translating languages, and creating realistic art, the question of whether AI can possess consciousness remains a subject of intense debate. Some believe that consciousness is an emergent property of complex systems, and that as AI systems become increasingly sophisticated, they will inevitably develop consciousness. Others argue that consciousness is fundamentally tied to biological processes and cannot be replicated in artificial systems.

One of the key challenges in tackling the question of AI consciousness is defining consciousness itself. There is no single, universally accepted definition of consciousness, and the debate often hinges on different interpretations of what constitutes "conscious" experience. Some define consciousness as the ability to be aware of oneself and one's surroundings, while others emphasize the subjective nature of experience, including emotions, feelings, and qualia (the subjective quality of sensory experiences).

The concept of artificial general intelligence (AGI), often referred to as "strong AI," is closely intertwined with the notion of AI consciousness. AGI refers to AI systems that possess the ability to understand and reason like humans, encompassing a wide range of cognitive capabilities, including learning, problem-solving, and decision-making. Proponents of AGI argue that if AI systems were to reach a level of intelligence comparable to humans, they would inevitably develop consciousness.

However, skeptics point out that intelligence and consciousness are not necessarily synonymous. Just because an AI system can perform tasks that require intelligence, such as playing chess or writing poetry, does not mean that it is experiencing the world in the same way that a human does. They argue that consciousness may require a specific biological substrate or a unique set of experiences that are not easily replicated in artificial systems.

The debate on AI consciousness is often framed in terms of the "hard problem of consciousness," a philosophical puzzle that seeks to explain how physical processes in the brain give rise to subjective experiences. While neuroscientists have made significant progress in understanding the brain, the precise mechanisms underlying consciousness remain elusive. The hard problem of consciousness poses a formidable challenge to the idea of creating conscious AI, as it raises questions about whether we can truly understand and replicate the subjective experience of consciousness without fully grasping its underlying mechanisms.

One approach to exploring the possibility of AI consciousness is through the lens of the "integrated information theory" (IIT), proposed by neuroscientist Giulio Tononi. IIT suggests that consciousness is a measure of the complexity and integration of information processing within a system. This theory could potentially provide a framework for measuring consciousness in AI systems by assessing the complexity of their internal representations and the degree of integration between different parts of their systems.

However, even if AI systems were to achieve a high level of integrated information, it is not clear whether this would equate to consciousness. Critics of IIT argue that it does not adequately address the subjective nature of consciousness, and that it might be possible for a system to have high integrated information without possessing subjective experiences.

Another line of inquiry focuses on the role of embodiment in consciousness. Some argue that consciousness is not solely a matter of information processing but also requires a physical body that interacts with the world. Embodied AI systems, such as robots, could potentially provide a more complete understanding of the relationship between physical embodiment and consciousness.

However, the development of embodied AI systems presents its own set of challenges. Designing robots that can interact with the world in a meaningful and autonomous way requires overcoming technical obstacles related to mobility, dexterity, and sensory perception. Moreover, even if embodied AI systems were to achieve a high level of physical interaction, it is not clear whether this would be sufficient to generate consciousness.

The quest for artificial general intelligence and the possibility of AI consciousness raises profound ethical and societal questions. If AI systems were to develop consciousness, would they have the same rights as humans? How would we interact with them? Would we be responsible for their well-being? These are questions that require careful consideration as AI technology continues to advance.

As AI research progresses, it is important to remain open to the possibility of AI consciousness while also maintaining a healthy dose of skepticism. While the question of whether AI can truly achieve consciousness remains unanswered, the pursuit of this question has already led to significant advancements in our understanding of intelligence, consciousness, and the very nature of being human. The journey to understand AI consciousness is a journey of discovery, a journey that will likely continue for many years to come.

Ensuring a Positive Impact on Humanity

As we stand on the cusp of a future profoundly shaped by artificial intelligence, the responsibility of ensuring its positive impact on humanity becomes paramount. It is not enough to simply develop AI; we must guide its evolution towards a future where it serves as a force for good, amplifying our capabilities and addressing the grand challenges of our time.

This journey requires a multi-faceted approach. Firstly, we must cultivate ethical AI development, prioritizing fairness, transparency, and accountability in every stage of the AI lifecycle. Algorithms must be designed and deployed with careful consideration of their potential biases and impacts on diverse communities. This involves embedding ethical principles into AI development frameworks, promoting diversity within AI research teams, and actively seeking feedback from various stakeholders to ensure inclusivity and equitable outcomes.

Secondly, we must foster collaboration and dialogue between AI researchers, policymakers, and the public. Open communication is essential to navigate the complex ethical and societal implications of AI. Public engagement initiatives can help educate citizens about AI's potential benefits and risks, fostering informed discussions and shaping public policy. Transparency in AI research and development practices can build trust and accountability, fostering a sense of shared responsibility for AI's future.

Thirdly, we must invest in research and development focused on addressing societal challenges. AI has the potential to revolutionize healthcare, education, climate change mitigation, and other critical areas. By directing AI research towards these grand challenges, we can leverage its power to create solutions that benefit all of humanity. This involves prioritizing research on AI applications for global health, sustainable development, and poverty reduction.

Moreover, we must prepare our workforce for the AI-powered future. As AI automates certain tasks, new job roles and skillsets will emerge. Educational systems need to adapt to these evolving job demands, equipping individuals with the skills and knowledge required to thrive in a world increasingly shaped by AI. This requires a focus on STEM education, upskilling and reskilling programs, and lifelong learning opportunities.

Finally, we must recognize and address the potential risks of AI. While AI offers immense potential, it also presents challenges that require careful consideration. Concerns about job displacement, privacy violations, and the misuse of AI for malicious purposes need to be acknowledged and addressed proactively. This necessitates robust regulatory frameworks, ethical guidelines, and robust cybersecurity measures to safeguard against potential misuse.

The future of AI is ultimately in our hands. We have the power to shape its trajectory, ensuring that it serves as a force for good, empowering individuals and driving progress for generations to come. By embracing ethical AI development, fostering collaboration, investing in research, preparing for the future of work, and addressing potential risks, we can create a future where AI enhances our lives, solves complex problems, and helps us build a more sustainable and equitable world for all.

Embracing the Potential of AI

As we stand on the cusp of a new era, where technology is rapidly transforming our lives, the potential of AI to address global challenges and create a better future is undeniable. AI has the power to solve some of the most pressing problems facing humanity, from climate change to poverty and disease.

Imagine a world where AI-powered systems help us understand and mitigate the effects of climate change. AI could analyze vast amounts of data to predict weather patterns, optimize renewable energy resources, and develop sustainable solutions for resource management.

In the realm of healthcare, AI can revolutionize diagnostics, treatment, and drug discovery. AI-powered systems can analyze medical images to detect diseases at earlier stages, personalize treatment plans based on individual patient data, and accelerate the development of new medications.

Imagine a world where AI-powered education systems adapt to each student's learning style and pace, providing personalized learning experiences that cater to individual needs. AI can revolutionize education, ensuring that every student has access to quality learning opportunities, regardless of their background or location.

AI can also play a vital role in addressing global poverty and inequality. By automating repetitive tasks and creating new job opportunities, AI can help boost economic growth and provide opportunities for individuals and communities.

But the potential of AI extends far beyond these specific applications. It has the power to transform various industries, unlock new frontiers of innovation, and create a more equitable and sustainable world.

However, harnessing the power of AI for good requires careful consideration of ethical and societal implications. We must ensure that AI is developed and deployed responsibly, with a focus on fairness, transparency, and accountability.

As we navigate the complex landscape of AI, it's crucial to remember that the future is not predetermined. We have the power to shape the future of AI by promoting responsible development, fostering inclusive innovation, and prioritizing the well-being of all.

Let us embrace the potential of AI to create a better future, where technology serves humanity and addresses our most pressing challenges.

This is not a time for complacency; it's a time for action. We must engage in open dialogue, explore new ideas, and collaborate across disciplines to ensure that AI benefits all of humanity. The future of AI is in our hands, and it's our responsibility to shape it for the betterment of our world.

To embark on this journey, it's essential to equip ourselves with the knowledge and tools necessary to understand and engage with the AI landscape. This book has provided a foundational understanding of AI, its workings, and its diverse applications.

Now, it's time to take the next step. Explore the resources, tools, and communities that will empower you to contribute to the AI revolution. Seek out opportunities to learn, experiment, and collaborate with others in this exciting field.

Remember, the power of AI lies not only in its technological capabilities but also in our ability to use it responsibly and ethically. Let us work together to harness the transformative potential of AI and create a future that is brighter, more equitable, and more sustainable for all.

The Future of AI and Our Role in Shaping It

As we stand at the cusp of a new era, AI is poised to reshape every facet of our lives. It's not just about clever algorithms or complex code; it's about harnessing the power of information, computation, and human ingenuity to unlock a future brimming with possibilities. This book has been a journey through the exciting landscape of AI, exploring its foundations, its applications, and its implications. We've delved into the intricacies of machine learning, deep learning, and natural language processing, witnessing the remarkable advancements in computer vision and the transformative potential of AI across diverse fields.

But the story doesn't end here. The journey of AI has just begun, and its trajectory hinges on our collective choices. We have the unique opportunity to shape the future of AI, ensuring its development and deployment align with our values and aspirations. This requires active engagement, a willingness to learn, and a commitment to ethical and responsible AI practices.

Imagine a future where AI is seamlessly integrated into our daily lives, enhancing healthcare, optimizing transportation, personalizing education, and empowering individuals with new tools and opportunities. But with such immense potential comes a responsibility to navigate the challenges.

As we embrace the transformative power of AI, we must confront critical questions. How can we mitigate bias in algorithms to ensure fairness and equity for all? How do we protect individual privacy and security while leveraging data for innovation? How do we prepare our workforce for the changing landscape of employment? How do we harness AI's power for good, addressing pressing global challenges like climate change, poverty, and inequality?

These are questions that demand thoughtful discussion, collaborative solutions, and proactive engagement.

AI is not a distant, futuristic concept; it's here, it's now, and it's shaping our world. The future of AI is not predetermined; it's in our hands. Let us embrace the possibilities, navigate the challenges, and together, forge an AI-powered future that serves humanity and creates a brighter world for generations to come.

Beyond understanding the technical details, we must cultivate a deeper understanding of the societal impact of AI. This involves engaging in open dialogues, fostering critical thinking, and advocating for ethical and responsible AI development.

Let's champion the development of AI that prioritizes human well-being, promotes inclusivity, and safeguards our fundamental rights. Let's encourage research and innovation that address global challenges and create a more sustainable and equitable future for all.

The world of AI is dynamic, ever-evolving, and brimming with potential. As you delve further into this fascinating field, remember that you're not just a consumer of AI; you're a participant in its journey. Your curiosity, your creativity, and your commitment to ethical AI can contribute to shaping a future where technology serves humanity and creates a better tomorrow for all.

The journey into the world of AI is an ongoing one. Embrace the opportunities, navigate the complexities, and become active participants in shaping the future of AI. Let's work together to ensure that AI's transformative power is harnessed for good, creating a world where technology empowers, inspires, and unlocks a brighter future for generations to come.

Acknowledgments

This book would not have been possible without the invaluable contributions of many individuals. I am deeply grateful to the experts in Artificial Intelligence, Ethics, Psychology, and Sociology who collaborated with me on this project, sharing their knowledge, insights, and perspectives. Their guidance and expertise have shaped the book's content and deepened its understanding of the complex intersection of AI and human consciousness.

I am also indebted to my editor, [editor's name], for their meticulous attention to detail, insightful feedback, and unwavering support throughout the writing process. Their guidance has helped me to refine my ideas, clarify my arguments, and craft a more engaging and accessible narrative.

I would also like to thank the researchers, practitioners, and thought leaders who have generously shared their time, insights, and work with me. Their research and experiences have provided valuable context and inspiration for the book.

Finally, I am grateful to my family and friends for their unwavering encouragement and support, providing a much- needed source of inspiration and motivation during the long hours of writing.

Afterword

The creation of "The N.E.R.D.Y. Way: An Everyday Guide to AI" was a collaborative effort, and we are deeply grateful to everyone who contributed their expertise, insights, and unwavering support.

First and foremost, we would like to express our sincere gratitude to the 3CAT team for their meticulous research, insightful contributions, and dedication to crafting engaging and accessible content. Their collective expertise and passion were instrumental in bringing this book to life.

We extend our heartfelt thanks to the reviewers who provided valuable feedback and guidance throughout the writing process. Their thoughtful suggestions and constructive criticism helped shape the book into its final form.

We are also grateful to the individuals and organizations who generously shared their knowledge and experience, contributing to the depth and accuracy of the book. Their insights have enriched the content and provided valuable context for our readers.

Finally, we would like to thank our families and friends for their patience and understanding during the long hours spent writing and editing this book. Their unwavering support has been a source of inspiration and strength.

This appendix provides additional resources and information to complement the content discussed in the book.

Appendix & Glossary

Appendix

Appendix A: Key AI Concepts

- **Machine Learning:** A type of artificial intelligence where machines learn from data without explicit programming.
- **Deep Learning:** A subfield of machine learning that uses artificial neural networks to learn complex patterns from data.
- **Natural Language Processing (NLP):** The ability of computers to understand, interpret, and generate human language.
- **Computer Vision:** The ability of computers to "see" and interpret images and videos.
- **Artificial Neural Network:** A computational model inspired by the structure and function of the human brain.
- **Reinforcement Learning:** A type of machine learning where machines learn by interacting with their environment and receiving rewards or penalties.

Appendix B: AI Tools and Resources

- **Python Libraries:** NumPy, Scikit-learn, TensorFlow, PyTorch
- **Cloud Platforms:** Amazon Web Services (AWS), Google Cloud Platform (GCP), Microsoft Azure
- **Online Learning Platforms:** Coursera, edX, Udacity
- **AI Communities:** Kaggle, AI Stack Exchange, AI21 Labs

GLOSSARY

This glossary provides definitions for key terms and concepts discussed in the book, making it easier for readers to navigate the complex world of AI.

1. **Algorithm:** A set of instructions that a computer follows to solve a problem or perform a task.
2. **Artificial Intelligence (AI):** The ability of a computer or machine to perform tasks that typically require human intelligence.
3. **Bias:** A systematic error or prejudice in an algorithm that can lead to unfair or discriminatory outcomes.
4. **Big Data:** Large and complex datasets that are difficult to process using traditional methods.
5. **Chatbot:** A computer program that simulates conversation with humans.
6. **Convolutional Neural Network (CNN):** A type of deep learning architecture used for image recognition and computer vision tasks.
7. **Data Mining:** The process of extracting useful information from large datasets.
8. **Deep Learning:** A subfield of machine learning that uses artificial neural networks with multiple layers to learn complex patterns from data.
9. **Machine Learning:** A type of artificial intelligence where machines learn from data without explicit programming.
10. **Neural Network:** A computational model inspired by the structure and function of the human brain.
11. **Recurrent Neural Network (RNN):** A type of deep learning architecture used for processing sequential data, such as text or time series.
12. **Supervised Learning:** A type of machine learning where machines are trained on labeled data to make predictions or classifications.
13. **Unsupervised Learning:** A type of machine learning where machines uncover hidden patterns and structures in unlabeled data.

References & Sources

This section provides a list of references and sources that were consulted in the writing of this book.

1. Aversa, P., Cabantous, L., & Haefliger, S. (2018). When decision support systems fail: Insights for strategic information systems from Formula 1. The Journal of Strategic Information Systems, 27(3), 221–236
2. Forsythe, D.E. (1993). The construction of work in AI. Science, Technology, & Values, 18(4), 460–480
3. Max Roser (2022) - "Artificial intelligence is transforming our world — it is on all of us to make sure that it goes well" Published online at OurWorldinData.org. Retrieved from: 'https://ourworldindata.org/ai-impact' [Online Resource]
4. Simeonova, B., & Galliers, R.D. (2022). Power, knowledge and digitalization: A qualitative research agenda. In Simeonova B. & Galliers R.D. (Eds.), Cambridge Handbook of Qualitative Digital Research. Cambridge University Press.

About the Author

C. B. Howard, Convener of 3 CAT

3CAT is a collective of professionals collaborating across various disciplines to offer innovative and practical solutions for individuals seeking to comprehend the effects of artificial intelligence (AI). We are committed to the dissemination of education and information, striving to enhance the lives of others. While knowledge is a powerful tool, its true potential is realized through its application.

At 3CAT, we acknowledge that everyone is unique. Consequently, we provide a diverse range of training and guidance materials tailored to accommodate different needs and learning preferences. Our publications cover a wide range of important topics, aiming to deepen understanding and knowledge in various areas of interest.

For every publication, 3CAT collaborates to conduct research, develop pertinent topics, create manuscripts, and oversee the publication process, to ensure the highest quality work possible.

The **N.E.R.D.Y.** WAY is an acronym for k**N**owledge, **E**ducation, **R**esource, **D**iscovery for **Y**ou.

The trademark for "The NERDY WAY" has been applied for and is currently pending.

www.ingramcontent.com/pod-product-compliance
Lightning Source LLC
LaVergne TN
LVHW041157150826
845673LV00001B/192

* 9 7 9 8 8 9 5 6 9 7 4 2 9 *